CW01501403

CONTENTS

LETTERS FOR THE AGES: GREAT MUSICIANS

Edited by James Drake
Edward Smyth

BLOOMSBURY CONTINUUM
LONDON • OXFORD • NEW YORK • NEW DELHI • SYDNEY

BLOOMSBURY CONTINUUM
Bloomsbury Publishing Plc
50 Bedford Square, London, WC1B 3DP, UK
Bloomsbury Publishing Ireland Limited
29 Earlsfort Terrace, Dublin 2, D02 AY28, Ireland

BLOOMSBURY, BLOOMSBURY CONTINUUM and the Diana logo are trademarks of
Bloomsbury Publishing Plc

First published in Great Britain 2025

A catalogue record for this book is available from the British Library

Library of Congress Cataloguing-in-Publication data has been applied for

ISBN: HB: 978-1-3994-1946-8; eBook: 978-1-3994-1948-2; ePDF: 978-1-3994-1949-9

2 4 6 8 10 9 7 5 3 1

Typeset by Deanta Global Publishing Services, Chennai, India
Printed and bound in Great Britain by Clays Ltd, Elcograf S.p.A.

To find out more about our authors and books visit www.bloomsbury.com
and sign up for our newsletters

For product safety related questions contact productsafety@bloomsbury.com

LETTERS FOR THE AGES:
GREAT MUSICIANS

ACKNOWLEDGEMENTS

Creating the book you hold in your hands has been a remarkable journey, made possible by the tireless efforts and generous contributions of numerous individuals.

Firstly, we must acknowledge the rights holders who have so generously given us permission to reproduce the letters included in this volume, and Helen Bartlett for her essential role in connecting us with them. Their willingness to share these letters has provided the book with a rich tapestry of experiences and stories.

We would also like to extend our sincere gratitude to David Pickard and Mark Wigglesworth for writing the introductory essays for this volume. Their passion and support for the project have been remarkable, and we are delighted to be able to share their insights with readers. Our thanks must also go to Edward Smyth for writing such a compelling narrative which has brought the stories hidden within the letters themselves to life.

Equally, we are incredibly grateful to our editors at Bloomsbury Continuum, whose support and editorial guidance have been integral to the continuation of the Letters for the Ages series.

We would also like to thank our researchers Lydia Higman and Benjamin Little for their assistance locating many of these letters.

The Of Lost Time team deserves special recognition for bringing the book to life. First, to John Sandy-Hindmarch for taking the seedling of an idea and making it bloom; his passion and insight are woven into this book's every page. And also to Isabel Jacob and Danny Al-Khafaji for their project management and countless hours spent casting an analytical eye over the book.

EDITORIAL CONVENTIONS

The letters in this book were penned by dozens of authors, each with a distinct voice and flair. In order to print this collection we have edited some of the letters to our house style, while trying to maintain the authenticity and individuality of each author.

Spelling mistakes (intentional or not) have been kept in the letters for authenticity of voice and are indicated by the inclusion of [*sic*] beside the word.

We have identified where the author has omitted words of their own text by striking through the text ~~like so.~~

Capitalization, italicization and underlining have been reproduced as they are in the text.

Some of the featured letters are too lengthy to print in their entirety, so some editorial cuts have had to be made for clarity; these are indicated by an ellipsis (. . .). Simultaneously, we have chosen to expand certain words that are abbreviated in the original text for clarity and ease of reading.

For readers interested in seeing the letters in full, please see the appendix of literature and sources at the back of the book or contact us at info@oflosttime.com.

FOREWORD

Over the 40-odd years that I have been working in the arts I have witnessed huge changes in the way musicians and administrators communicate. My very first job offer, in 1982 as assistant to the company manager at the Royal Opera House, came on a telegram. When I worked on a big Japanese Festival in 1991 we laughed that it could never have happened without the invention of the fax machine. Fee negotiations at Glyndebourne moved, in the first decade of the twenty-first century, from exchanges of letters to long email trails. And now a Proms programme is invariably wrapped up with a smiley emoji on a WhatsApp. But I still admire the many composers who write a good, old-fashioned letter (with enclosed score) to try to tempt the Proms into performing their latest work. And I treasure the Christmas cards I used to receive from that great, workaholic conductor Charles Mackerras, who always included his schedule for the following year – pointing out the tiny gaps when he was free to take on extra engagements.

This marvellous collection of letters reveals striking similarities in the preoccupations of musicians over time, forming a bridge from the sixth to the twenty-first century. Despite their genius, great artists are real people; sometimes that endears them to us, but it can also shatter some illusions. I will never forget the uproar when, in *Amadeus*, Peter Shaffer portrayed Mozart (entirely convincingly) as an immature buffoon with a scatological sense of humour, and we find it hard to reconcile the genius of Wagner with his deeply unpleasant character. But does that make their music any less worthy?

One of the great privileges of running the Proms has been the opportunity to see both the private and public sides of the many musicians who take part. The beaming conductor walking off the stage after a performance, buoyed by an ovation from the audience. The soloist, pale with fear, furiously doing last-minute practice before going on to play a concerto. The composer who vents their frustration when an orchestra struggles with the fiendishly difficult music they have written. The good, the bad and the ugly. I've also been lucky enough to know some of them as friends as well as musicians, and to enjoy the jokes, worries, gossip, ups and downs that are all part of ordinary life.

The question we might ask as listeners is, should the personality of an artist or composer affect the way we listen to their music? And should what we hear be influenced by the personal circumstances under which a piece was written? I would say not. One of the joys of listening to music is that, because it is a largely abstract art form, we are at liberty to impose our own feelings and emotions on what we hear, without knowing what the artist felt when they were creating it. Even the common acceptance that major keys are happy and minor ones are sad is frequently undercut by music that contradicts this. And we try to second-guess a composer's musical intentions from their writings or personal life at our peril. For years we took at face value the statement from Shostakovich that his Symphony No. 5 was 'an artist's response to fair criticism' following personal attacks on his work from Stalin. Now there is a contrary view: that this is the bitter, angry and desperate reaction to the brutal regime under which he was living. Many composers have created their sunniest music at a time of deep personal crisis. And surely one definition of a genius is that you see and hear their work in different ways according to your own mood at the time. That's certainly the case with me and Mozart.

So we can enjoy reading these letters as a fascinating insight into the characters of extraordinary people most of us have not had the opportunity to meet. But they also show us that our heroes are, ultimately, human beings just like us, with the same joys, fears and frustrations that we all experience. They speak to us through their music; the astonishing legacy that has enriched my life, alongside millions of others.

David Pickard

INTRODUCTION

Much has been written about the expressive capabilities of words and music and how they differ as a means of communication. Some people think music has far too much emotional complexity to be adequately described in words. Others believe that words are less open to misinterpretation. This magnificently wide-ranging compilation of letters invites us to engage in the best of both worlds. It vividly illuminates the musicians behind the music, reminding us that they were relatively normal people, whose musical achievements therefore seem all the more remarkable.

There is a certain validity to the argument that the less we know about our musical heroes the better. Bringing them down to earth can inhibit music's almost supernatural power to transport us to the limit of our imaginations. But at its most fundamental level, music is a human activity, written by real people, for real people, about real people. It evolved as a means of communication, of telling stories, and of connecting us to each other in a way that creates compassion and encourages empathy. Letters bring people together too, and as third-party readers we are brought into the loop, closer to the writers, and thus closer to their music.

Performers have a duty of care to the composers of the music we study, constantly trying to understand better the emotions we are called upon to express. That process is, to a certain extent, made easier by knowing more about what composers were going through at the time they were writing their music. It is not that there is always a link between events in their lives and the music they produce – sometimes the very opposite seems to be the case.

But by being more connected to these musicians as human beings, we are more connected to the humanity of their music. And for most of us it is the humanity, rather than the musicianship, that we have in common. Composers create things we mere performers could never begin to attempt, but the experiences they describe are ones we all share. It is through this connection that we can try to be the conduits through which they speak.

As musicians, the writers of these letters could not be more different. I wonder if any other book has referenced Amy Winehouse and Hildegard of Bingen alongside Gustav Mahler and Elvis Presley. (Now there's a dinner party guest list if ever there was one!) Yet though on a musical level these writers could not be more different, these letters show how broadly similar they all are as people. And how similar to us too. Whatever our musical tastes, we can find personal connections to them all. Music is written by people who share the same day-to-day concerns as the rest of us, the same insecurities and vanities, needs and hopes, frustrations and joys. Given that the collection spans over 15 centuries of Western civilization, it appears the issues we care about don't seem to have changed much over time. Music has evolved to an almost unrecognizable degree; not so the humanity it seeks to express.

The majority of these letters were intended as private communications, and yet despite that, there can be a guarded quality to them, a certain self-consciousness even. 'A person has to be careful about writing letters,' Brahms once said. 'One day they get printed!' On the other hand, composers write their music for everyone to hear. They are open and fearless, perhaps feeling safer expressing themselves through music, within which they trust themselves to mean exactly what they say, than through words, where they are all too aware of the possibility of being misunderstood. Maybe they know that music's potential for ambiguity offers a certain degree of protection. I actually think there is nothing emotionally ambiguous about a highly specific combination of melody, harmony, rhythm and colour. But though music depicts feelings precisely, it is impossible to accurately translate what they are. This safety net enables outpourings that reveal the very deepest, at times darkest, places of the soul. We as listeners can go to those places too, similarly safe in the knowledge that no-one else can truly define where it is we are. We discover a common unity that embraces the fact that music, like humanity, is one world. Connected threads from which one can grasp comfort and inspiration.

Mark Wigglesworth

CHAPTER ONE

GENESIS OF THE GREATS

'My dad is content to sing loudly in his office and sell windows,' writes a 12-year-old Amy Winehouse in the last letter of this opening chapter. For her, the letter makes clear contentment could only be found through fame – and the knowledge that she had used the talent with which she had been 'blessed' to help people 'forget their troubles for five minutes'. Fame did not bring contentment, of course, and Winehouse was dead only 15 years later, a victim of the troubles her music had assuaged in the hearts of so many others. Hers was a short life and a tragic life. But it was also one of *greatness*.

What make a musician 'great'? There is no concise answer: it is a constellation of things – talent, charisma, imagination, determination, luck, timing – which, if found in the right combination in a single person, might just lead to success and from there on to greatness. But we tend to know whatever it is when we see it (the premise of many a TV talent show, including the one which references this 'X-factor' explicitly). And so for every 'great' there are hundreds or thousands or perhaps millions of talented musicians who once dreamed of stardom but in whom the ingredients for greatness were minutely out of proportion and who now, perhaps while selling windows, sing loudly in their offices.

To what extent 'name recognition' is a necessary constituent element of 'greatness' is up for debate. Christoph Willibald Gluck is not perhaps a household name in the same way as some of his contemporaries – Handel and Mozart, to name just a couple. He was certainly revered by some, though: Hector Berlioz regarded Gluck as, along with Beethoven, one of the 'two supreme gods in the art of music'. But Berlioz identified Gluck's greatness not primarily in his compositional ability, but rather in his sensitive and thoughtful approach to loosening some of the strictures and common practices of the composition of opera which he felt were suffocating the form. Well-known? Not particularly. Great? Without question.

An endearing press release launched the Ramones onto an unsuspecting world in 1975. Laced with a touch of humour ('Their sound is not unlike a fast drill on a rear molar'), it nevertheless got their message across ('the songs are brief, to the point and every one a potential hit single'); and was borne out by the success and longevity of the group, which finally disbanded in 1996. By 2014 all four members named in this press release were dead, but the Ramones were established in the pantheon of the greats.

As great responsibility is the obligation of power, so great misery often seems to be the obligation of greatness. This is more than adequately illustrated by those whose letters we read in this chapter – a chapter with representation from that most miserable group of greats: the so-called '27 Club'. Needless to say, a predisposition to the kinds of emotional and physical problems which seem so disproportionately to affect 'the great' is not in itself a prerequisite for greatness, but the fact it seems so common should give us pause for thought, especially in a society which seems increasingly incapable of recognizing or respecting the notion of privacy.

We will return to the idea of privacy – and the extent to which it is demanded and sacrificed – later. Suffice to say that the way the public relates to someone we class as 'great' has changed beyond all recognition in the time between the earliest letter of this chapter – from Mozart – and the latest – that of Amy Winehouse. To express any sympathy for those whose every step and, crucially, every misstep is taken in the public eye is generally to invite a response along the lines of 'Small price to pay for fame and fortune,' or 'They brought it upon themselves.' This is unduly unsympathetic, as some of the letters in the chapter serve to illustrate.

This first chapter closes with the young Amy Winehouse complaining of her father's lack of ambition. Ambition is perhaps the running theme of the first eight letters of this book, explicit or implicit. But we cannot turn the page on this chapter without a nagging doubt – a residual concern – that one ought to be careful what one wishes for. The life of greatness is one achieved by very few indeed, but for many of that few it is not an easy life and often not a long one either. There is a cost, then, to greatness; a price to be paid. A price worth paying? Only those who have paid it could answer that. As we read the letters which follow from the greats 'before they were famous', then, we might do so listening carefully for the humanity which seems so often to find itself overwhelmed – utterly erased – by the unstoppable tide of 'greatness'.

As for us non-greats? Well, for us it is those greats whose music fills our lives with joy, and those greats who inspire us in turn to strive towards our own kind of greatness.

'THE WHOLE THEATRE WAS SO CRAMMED THAT MANY PEOPLE WERE OBLIGED TO GO AWAY'

MOZART LAPS UP THE APPLAUSE

Mozart is a name recognizable even to those with the most rudimentary knowledge of or interest in classical music. Compositions such as his Requiem, Symphony No. 41 and *The Marriage of Figaro* (to name but a few) remain some of the best loved pieces of classical music ever, and tourists continue to flock to Salzburg to visit the birthplace of Austria's most influential musician over 200 years after his death.

The genesis of this true musical great is in keeping with the mythos that surrounds him. By the age of 18 Wolfgang Amadeus Mozart (1756–91) had travelled the length and breadth of Europe, performing in both the continent's most prestigious concert halls and the royal courts of Kings Louis XV of France, George III of England and William V, Prince of Orange and Stadtholder of the Dutch Republic. He had also brushed shoulders with many of the most influential figures in the European music scene.

His early compositions – which, by his sister Maria Anna's account, he began to produce from the tender age of five – included numerous arias, sonatas, operas and a symphony. By the mid-1770s Mozart had undoubtedly already established himself as one of the most exciting composers in European music, and it was with the intention of capitalizing on this already enviable reputation that in December of 1774 Mozart travelled to Munich.

He timed his arrival to coincide with the start of the city's carnival season, hoping to give his brand-new opera *La finta giardiniera* the best chance of being staged. Though this was already his ninth opera it was also only his second attempt at writing an opera buffa (a genre of comic opera), and Mozart's proficiency in this discipline remained to be seen. After a successful set of rehearsals for the production, however, Mozart was full of confidence as he eagerly awaited the big day of its debut.

Much to his relief, the opera's opening night did not disappoint, and he wrote a touching letter to his mother Anna Maria (along with their beloved dog, Bimperl) back in Salzburg to share the news.

Despite the successful debut, *La finta giardiniera* did not result in the gainful employment Mozart had hoped for. Instead, he would have to wait until 1781 when he travelled to Vienna before he could realize his potential. He would spend the rest of his life in the city, and here would create his legacy as one of the all-time greats.

A MOZART FAMILY PORTRAIT PAINTED BY JOHANN CROCE, *C.*1781

From Wolfgang Amadeus Mozart to Anna Maria Mozart, 1775

Munich, January 14, 1775

God be praised! My opera was given yesterday, the 13th, and proved so successful that I cannot possibly describe all the tumult. In the first place, the whole theatre was so crammed that many people were obliged to go away. After each aria there was invariably a tremendous uproar and clapping of hands, and cries of *Viva Maestro!* Her Serene Highness the Electress and the Dowager (who were opposite me) also called out Bravo! When the opera was over, during the interval when all is usually quiet till the ballet begins, the applause and shouts of *Bravo!* were renewed; sometimes there was a lull, but only to recommence afresh, and so forth. I afterwards went with papa to a room through which the Elector and the whole court were to pass. I kissed the hands of the Elector and the Electress and the other royalties, who were all very gracious. At an early hour this morning the Prince Bishop of Chiemsee sent to congratulate me that the opera had proved such a brilliant success in every respect. As to our return home, it is not likely to be soon, nor should mamma wish it, for she must know well what a good thing it is to have a little breathing-time. We shall come quite soon enough to—. One most just and undeniable reason is, that my opera is to be given again on Friday next, and I am very necessary at the performance, or it might be difficult to recognize it again. There are very odd ways here. 1,000 kisses to Miss Bimberl

'I AGREE WITH YOU THAT OF ALL MY COMPOSITIONS, *ORFEO* ALONE IS TOLERABLE; I SINCERELY BESEECH THE GOD OF TASTE TO FORGIVE ME FOR DEAFENING MY HEARERS WITH MY OTHER OPERAS'

GLUCKISTS VERSUS PICCINNISTS – THE BATTLE OF
THE OPERAS

In 1779, Parisian high society was in the throes of a full-blown culture war fought in newspaper pages and salons across the city, as well as within the Palace of Versailles itself. The cause? Two polarizing notions of how the opera of the future should sound.

On one side were the 'Piccinnists', a fanatical faction of fans of the Italian composer Niccolò Piccinni (1728–1800). The Piccinnists shared a Baroque philosophy, arguing that good opera was defined by scores full of elaborate instrumentals and acrobatic singing – in Italian, of course, the true language of opera.

In the opposing camp were the so called 'Gluckists', that is, the followers of the composer Christoph Willibald Gluck (1714–87), a German composer who had arrived on the Parisian scene earlier that decade and immediately caught the attention of the new Dauphine of France, Marie Antoinette. The Gluckists found the flamboyant, Baroque, Italian operatic style lacking: the music was overblown, the characters were superficial ciphers. Gluck believed he could reinvigorate the elegance of opera by stripping it back to its roots, thus reinstating the equilibrium between music and poetry; he also opposed the monopoly the Italian language held over opera, and argued for holding performances in French instead. Gluck, his ardent followers believed, would be the antidote that would return opera to its former musical glory.

In reality, neither Piccinni nor Gluck themselves were ever personally at odds, though this did not deter their supporters from sniping at one another at every opportunity. In this letter we can see Gluck's clash with one particularly strong exponent of the Piccinnist style, Jean-François de La Harpe. Harpe was a man of colourful reputation, described by one nineteenth-century biographer as 'the most stupid of all the stupid littérateurs who wrote about music'.

Having attended a performance of Gluck's operatic rendition of *Iphigenia in Aulis* earlier in 1777, Harpe decided to air his critical opinion in his *Journal de politique et de littérature*, attacking the opera for its lack of 'melody' and 'nobility'. Not one to take criticism lightly, Gluck decided to respond directly. Perhaps, he suggests in this letter, Harpe might be best to leave the production of music to the professionals.

From Christoph Willibald Gluck to Jean-François de La Harpe, 1777

October 1777

. . . It is impossible for me, Sir, to resist the very judicious observations you have just made upon my operas in your *Journal de Littérature* of the 5ᵗʰ of this month; I find nothing, absolutely nothing, to object against them.

Until now I had been so simple as to believe that music was like the other arts in that all passions fell within its province and that it should give no less pleasure by expressing the heat of one enraged or the cry of one in grief, than by rendering the sights of a lover.

I believe this maxim to be true in music as in poetry. I had persuaded myself that song, coloured through and through by the sentiments it was required to express, must change with them and take as many different accents as they had different shades; in short that the voice, the instruments, all sounds, even pauses, should be directed towards a single aim, that of expression, and that the union of words and singing should be so close that the poem would seem to be fitted to the music no less than the music to the song.

These were not my only errors; it appeared to me that the French language was lightly accented and had no fixed quantities like the Italian; I had been struck by another difference between the singers of the two nations. While I found the voices of the former to be softer and more pliant, the latter seemed to me to bring more vigour and action to their performance: I had concluded from this that the Italian style of singing was unsuitable for French voices. Thereafter, in looking through the scores of your old operas, despite the trills, cadenzas and other defects with which their airs seemed to me to be overloaded, I found in them sufficient real beauty to convince me that the French had their own resources to draw upon.

Those, Sir, were my ideas when I read your observations. But light immediately dispelled the darkness; I was confounded at perceiving that you had learnt more about my art in a few hours of reflection than I myself after practising it for forty years. You prove to me, Sir, that the man of letters can speak on any subject. I am now fully convinced that the music of the Italian masters is music *par excellence*, that it alone *is* music; that singing, if it is to please, must be regular and periodic, and that even in disordered moments, when the character who is singing, moved by a variety of passions, passes in succession from one to another, the composer must always preserve the same style.

I agree with you that of all my compositions, *Orfeo* alone is tolerable; I sincerely beseech the God of taste to forgive me for *deafening* my hearers with my other operas; the number of performances they have received and the applause the public has been good enough to bestow upon them do not prevent me from seeing that they are pitiful; I am so convinced of this that I wish to rewrite them; and as I perceive you to be in favour of tender airs, I shall place in the mouth of the angry Achilles a song so touching and so sweet that the whole audience will be moved to tears.

As for *Armide*, I shall take good care not to leave the poem as it is at present, for, as you so justly observe, *Quinault's operas, though full of beauties, are designed in a manner very little suited to music; they are very fine poems, but very bad operas*: so even if they should become very bad poems, the only question being to make fine operas after your manner, I implore you to make me acquainted with some versifier who can take Armide in hand and fit every scene with two airs. We shall agree together about the quantity and metre of the lines; so long as they have their full number of syllables I shall not concern myself with the rest. For my part I am working at the music, from which it goes without saying, I shall scrupulously banish all noisy instruments, such as the timpani and the trumpet; in my orchestra I wish only oboes, flutes, French horns and violins to be heard – with mutes, of course; all that will then remain will be to fit the words to the tunes, which will not be difficult, as we shall have taken our measurements beforehand . . .

. . . I am resolved not *to shock the ears* of M. de La Harpe, I am resolved not to *counterfeit nature*, I wish to *embellish* it, instead of causing Armide to *bawl*, I wish her to *enchant* you. Were he to persist, were he to point out to me that Sophocles, in the finest of his tragedies, was bold enough to bring Oedipus before the Athenians with bleeding eyes, and that the recitative, or species of intoned declamation, in which that unfortunate King expressed his eloquent laments must undoubtedly have been delivered in tones of the most acute distress, my reply will be, again, that M. de La Harpe does not wish to hear the *cries of a man in pain.*

Have I not well grasped, Sir, the spirit of the doctrine with which your observations are imbued? I have given several of my friends the pleasure of reading them. 'You ought to be grateful,' said one of them, on returning them to me. 'M. de La Harpe gives you some excellent hints, he makes his statement of musical policy; do the same for him; procure his poetical and literary works and, in friendship for him, call attention to everything that does not please you in them . . . It may be objected that it is unbecoming in you, a musician, to decide questions of poetry; but would that be more surprising than to find a poet, a man of letters, uttering a despotic judgement of music?'

So said my friend; his reasoning seems to me to be very sound; but despite my gratitude to you I feel, Sir, after fully considering the matter, that I cannot defer to it without incurring the fate of the dissertator who made a long speech on the art of war in the presence of Hannibal . . .

'IF THE PAPERS FLOG ME SO SOUNDLY THAT I CAN'T SHOW MYSELF IN PUBLIC I HAVE MADE UP MY MIND TO BECOME A HOUSE-DECORATOR'

FRÉDÉRIC CHOPIN RECOUNTS THE DAZZLING SUCCESS OF HIS FIRST LIVE PERFORMANCE

Freshly graduated from the Warsaw Conservatory, in July 1829 the 19-year-old Frédéric Chopin (1810–49) arrived in Vienna as a largely unknown musician. He had made the long journey from Poland to Austria in the company of three friends, all young graduates eager to brush shoulders with the music capital of Europe's 'great and good'. Above all, Chopin was keen to make the acquaintance of the Austrian composer and music publisher Tobias Haslinger, in the hope of convincing him to publish his compositions.

Haslinger was certainly impressed by Chopin's talent, but astounded to discover that he had not yet demonstrated his unique talents in public as an adult. Chopin had been performing since 1818 when he was just eight years old but, for various reasons, found the prospect of performing a solo concert in Austria 'incomprehensible', as he described it in a letter to his parents written that summer. Spurred on by Haslinger and his contemporaries, though, he eventually relented and made his debut performance at the Royal-Imperial Court Opera Theatre on 11 August 1829.

Chopin organized the repertoire with the help of the Czech composer and pianist Wilhelm Würfel. To begin, he would play Beethoven's overture introducing the ballet *The Creatures of Prometheus*. Next, the debut of his Op. 2 variations on *Là ci darem la mano*, which he had composed in 1827 at the age of 17. In 1831 the variations would be heard by the composer and critic Robert

Schumann, who was so moved by the performance that he wrote of Chopin, 'Hats off, gentleman, a genius.'

It is unclear which rondo Chopin intended to play, with opinion split between Op. 5, *Rondo à la Mazur*, and *Rondo à la Krakowiak*. On the back of a dreadful rehearsal of this piece, however, Chopin decided to make a last-minute change, resolving instead to play a fantasia, or improvisational piece. The first was an improvisation based on *La Dame Blanche* (The White Lady) by François-Adrien Boieldieu, a piece he had only heard for the first time a few nights earlier. Second was a *chmiel* – a raucous Polish drinking song – which proved a huge success with the bourgeois audience.

When the curtain fell on his Austrian debut, Chopin wrote this letter to his family, giddy with the triumph of his performance. The success of the debut was an astonishing achievement for such a young and inexperienced musician, especially given the whole event had been put together in just three days. Such audacity was a mark of Chopin's brilliance, and would set him in fine stead to become one of the greatest musicians of the nineteenth century.

ONE OF THE FEW SURVIVING PHOTOGRAPHS
OF FRÉDÉRIC CHOPIN, 1840s

From Frédéric Chopin to his family, 1829

Vienna. Wednesday 12 August 1829

From my previous letter you learned, my dearest parents, that I had allowed myself to be persuaded to give a concert; and so yesterday, Tuesday, at seven o'clock in the evening I made my bow on the stage of the Royal and Imperial Opera House! The sort of performance that took place yesterday in this theatre is called here a 'Musical Academy'. Since I got nothing out of it, and did not try to get anything, Count Gallenberg put it on quickly and arranged the programme thus:

A Beethoven Overture
My Variations
Song by Mlle Veltheim
My Rondo

then another song after which the evening ended with a short ballet. The orchestral accompaniment went so badly at rehearsal that I substituted a Free Fantasia for the Rondo. As soon as I appeared on the stage they started clapping; and the applause was so great after each variation that I could not hear the orchestral *tuttis*. At the end they applauded so loudly that I had to come back twice and bow. Although my Free Fantasia did not turn out particularly well they clapped still louder and I had to take another bow. I came out the more willingly since the appreciation of these Germans is worth something. Thus Würfel had brought to a successful conclusion on Tuesday a project that had only been thought of on Sunday: I am very much indebted to him.

It happened like this: on Saturday I made the acquaintance of Gyrowetz, Lachner, Kreutzer and Seyfried, and had a long conversation with Mayseder. As I was standing in front of the theatre, up comes Count Gallenberg and suggests that I should play on Tuesday. I agreed, and I have not been hissed off the stage! When I get back I will describe it all better than I can in writing. Don't worry about me and my reputation!

The journalists have taken me to their hearts; perhaps they will give me a few pin-pricks but that is necessary so as not to overdo the praise. Mr Demmar, the stage-manager, is particularly kind and pleasant to me. Before I went on he encouraged me so much by his reassurances and so took my mind off things that I had no trace of stage-fright, especially as the theatre was not full. My friends and colleagues distributed themselves among the audience in order to hear the various opinions and criticism. Celiński will tell you how little was said against me. Hube heard the worst: 'It is a pity the young man looks so unimpressive' – so declared one of the ladies. If that is the only fault they could find with me I have nothing to worry about. My friends swear they heard nothing but praise and they did not once have to give the sign for applause. I improvised on a theme from *La Dame Blanche*. Then the stage-manager begged me to choose another Polish theme – he liked my Rondo so much at rehearsal that after yesterday's concert he shook my hand warmly and said, 'Yes, the Rondo must be played here' – so I selected *Chmiel*, which electrified the public, unaccustomed as it is to this kind of melody. My spies on the floor of the house declare that people were dancing up and down in their seats.

Wertheim happened to arrive yesterday from Carlsbad with his wife and he came straight to the theatre. He couldn't at first realize that it was I who was playing; he came to congratulate me today. In Carlsbad he saw Hummel and says that Hummel asked after me and that he will write to Hummel today and tell him about my début. Haslinger is printing [the *Variations*, Opus 2]; I have kept a copy of the concert-poster.

The general opinion is that I played too quietly, or rather too delicately for those accustomed to the banging of the Viennese pianists. I expected to find such a reproach in the newspaper in view of the fact that the editor's daughter bangs the piano frightfully. It doesn't matter. There must always be some kind of 'but . . .' and I should prefer it to be that one rather than have it said that I play too loudly.

Count Dietrichstein, a member of the Imperial entourage, came behind stage and had a long conversation with me in French. He complimented me and advised me to stay longer in Vienna. The orchestra was up in arms over my bad musical handwriting and sulked until I began to improvise, whereupon they joined in the clapping and exclamations of the whole audience. I can see that the orchestra is on my side, although I don't yet know how things stand with the other musicians. There is no need for them to be unfriendly – they know I did not play for material gain.

So there you have my début, all the more successful since it was unexpected. Hube says that a man gets nowhere by following the common road and keeping to a prearranged plan. It's better to leave some things to chance. And so it was by the merest chance that I was persuaded to give a concert. If the papers flog me so soundly that I can't show myself in public I have made up my mind to become a house-decorator, for it is quite easy to run one's brush over the paper and one still remains a son of Apollo!

I am curious to know what Mr Elsner will say to all this; perhaps he is displeased that I have played? But they really insisted so much that I could not refuse. Besides, it seems to me that no harm has been done. Nidecki was extraordinarily obliging yesterday: he looked over and corrected the orchestral parts and was sincerely delighted at my success. I played on a Graff [sic] piano. Today I am wiser and more experienced by four years. How surprised you must have been to notice that I sealed my last letter with a seal taken from a bottle of Madeira! But I was so absent-minded that I picked up the first decent seal that came to hand – left behind by a waiter – and hastily stuck it on my letter.

'PROVIDED I DON'T GO MAD, YOU WILL FIND AN ARTIST IN ME!'

FRANZ LISZT RIDES THE HIGHS AND LOWS OF FRENZIED CREATIVITY

In 1844, a mania swept across the audiences of European concert halls. Symptoms included hysteria and delirium, with audience members – particularly women – appearing to be caught in a state of ecstasy.

The epidemic was first reported by Heinrich Heine in his overview for that year's concert season for the Parisian press. Heine was initially dismissive of the reports of afflicted audiences in Berlin. When he witnessed the spectacle first-hand in Italy, however, he was finally convinced that something quite extraordinary was taking place. The common denominator across all these cases of hysteria? They were occurring during the performances of the Hungarian pianist Franz Liszt (1811–86). Accordingly, Heine saw fit to coin the term 'Lisztomania' to describe this new phenomenon.

Even today Liszt's mastery of the piano is considered by many to be unmatched. His mania-inducing performances revolutionized the piano's reputation, from that of a background accompaniment to an instrument capable of captivating an audience for an entire evening. So exuberant was his style of playing that it was not uncommon for Liszt to break his piano strings, the remnants of which were fiercely fought over by audience members in search of mementos.

Equal to the scale of his performances was his skill as a virtuoso. Beyond playing pieces composed for the piano, Liszt also arranged symphonies for the piano, managing, to the audience's amazement, to replicate entire orchestras with just two hands. As if this was not impressive enough, Liszt played all of his own pieces entirely from memory.

Years of diligent practice preceded Liszt's rise to stardom. Though he was undoubtedly gifted with an innate musical ability, he was all too aware that this raw talent needed to be nurtured with committed study. In this pair of letters, we get an erratic account of the dizzy heights of creativity Liszt could reach as he honed his craft as a pianist. As he writes to the French playwright Pierre Wolff, we see Liszt in the throes of a creative outburst emblematic of the frenzied performances for which he would become famous. So too are we presented with the highs and lows of Liszt's wild bouts of musical fervour, as each letter presents the before and after of one of these episodes.

FRANZ LISZT, 1850S

From Franz Liszt to Pierre Wolff (Junior), 1832

Paris, May 2nd

Here is a whole fortnight that my mind and fingers have been working like two lost spirits – Homer, the Bible, Plato, Locke,

Byron, Hugo, Lamartine, Chateaubriand, Beethoven, Bach, Hummel, Mozart, Weber, are all around me. I study them, meditate on them, devour them with fury; besides this I practise four to five hours of exercises (3rds, 6ths, 8ths, tremolos, repetition of notes, cadences, etc., etc.). Ah! provided I don't go mad, you will find an artist in me! Yes, an artist such as you desire, such as is required nowadays!

'And I too am a painter!' cried Michael Angelo the first time he beheld a chef d'œuvre . . . Though insignificant and poor, your friend cannot leave off repeating those words of the great man ever since Paganini's last performance. René, what a man, what a violin, what an artist! Heavens! what sufferings, what misery, what tortures in those four strings!

. . .

From Franz Liszt to Pierre Wolff (Junior), 1832

May 8th

My good friend, it was in a paroxysm of madness that I wrote the above lines; a strain of work, wakefulness and those violent desires (for which you know me) had set my poor head aflame; I went from right to left, then from left to right (like a sentinel in the winter, freezing), singing, declaiming, gesticulating, crying out; in a word, I was delirious. Today the spiritual and the animal (to use the witty language of M. de Maistre) are a little more evenly balanced; for the volcano of the heart is not extinguished, but is working silently. — Until when? —

Address your letters to Monsieur Reidet, the receiver-general at the port of Rouen.

A thousand kind messages to the ladies Boissier. I will tell you some day the reasons which prevented me from starting for Geneva. On this subject I shall call you in evidence.

Bertini is in London; Madame Malibran is making her round of Germany; Messemaecker (how is he getting on?) is resting on his laurels at Brussels; Aguado has the illustrious *maëstro* Rossini in tow.

Messemaecker Ah-Hi-Oh-Hu!!!

'BUT MY KEENEST DESIRE, MY MOST ARDENT WISH, IS TO BECOME KNOWN MORE COMPLETELY (IF NOT BY THE MAJORITY OF THE PUBLIC, THEN AT LEAST BY AN ENLIGHTENED FEW)'

TCHAIKOVSKY HUMBLY INTRODUCES HIMSELF

PYOTR ILYICH TCHAIKOVSKY,
PHOTOGRAPH TAKEN LATE NINETEENTH CENTURY

In the winter of 1876, Pyotr Ilyich Tchaikovsky composed a letter to Édouard Colonne, the acclaimed conductor and head of the Association Artistique du Châtelet, one of Paris's most prestigious orchestras. At that time, Tchaikovsky (1840–93) had already begun to carve out a reputation for himself in the concert halls of

Russia, but his name was largely unfamiliar to audiences outside his homeland. The opportunity to connect with influential figures in Paris was critical for Tchaikovsky, as he sought to expand his reach and gain recognition for his compositions.

In his correspondence, Tchaikovsky expressed a passionate desire to share his music with a wider audience, believing that the enlightened music lovers of Paris would appreciate his artistic vision. With great humility and respect, he approached Colonne, acknowledging the prominence of both the conductor and his orchestra in the French music scene. Tchaikovsky proposed a concert dedicated exclusively to his works, emphasizing that the event would not be for profit but rather a heartfelt offering to the public.

The proposal proved fruitful, and Colonne conducted the first performances of many of Tchaikovsky's works in Paris, including the Piano Concerto No. 1, Symphony No. 4, and the fantasia *The Tempest*. In fact, the pair shared such great mutual respect that on occasion Colonne even yielded his position to Tchaikovsky, allowing him to conduct his orchestra – a role he rarely entrusted to anyone.

This letter signifies a critical juncture in Tchaikovsky's career, marking his first earnest attempt to establish connections within Europe's vibrant musical landscape. It reflects not only his artistic ambitions but also his commitment to making his music accessible to all. With succinct clarity, Tchaikovsky's request for assistance reveals both his passion as a composer and the vulnerability that accompanies the pursuit of recognition in the arts.

From Pyotr Ilyich Tchaikovsky to Édouard Colonne, 1876

Moscow, 25 December 1876 / 6 January 1877

Monsieur!
I do not know if my name has the privilege of being known to you.

I am a Russian composer, resident in Moscow, enjoying a certain reputation in my country, but until now almost completely unknown abroad.

This winter Monsieur Pasdeloup played one of my overtures at one of his popular concerts. It seems that this work, although it caused some catcalls, did not pass unnoticed. Many musicians have written to me to say that they find my music rather interesting. But my keenest desire, my most ardent wish, — is to become known more completely (if not by the majority of the public, then at least by an enlightened few), Monsieur de Saint-Saëns told me last year that it might be possible, were I to contact you and to request for the assistance of your excellent orchestra as well as its eminent leader, — that you would perhaps have the extreme kindness to consent to interpret my compositions during a concert I might give in Paris.

And so, Monsieur, this is the substance of my request. I should like in March of this year to hire one of the concert halls of Paris and put on a concert made up exclusively of my works. As the aim of this concert is by no means financial gain, and as I would not presume to imagine that the public would pay to attend, — I would bring with me to Paris the sum necessary to pay the orchestra, the expenses of the concert hall and lighting, and I would distribute free tickets to all those in Paris who are interested in music. And so I beg you, Monsieur Colonne, to do me the honour of informing me:

1   if I might hope that you and your orchestra would be available for this projected concert;
2   what the charge would be for the orchestra (for three rehearsals and the concert);
3   what the charge would be for the concert hall, the notices, and the other expenses;
4   who I might contact to organize the arrangements.

I hope, Sir, you will not think badly of me for taking the liberty of addressing you directly, and, hoping that you will honour me with a response, I ask you, Monsieur, to accept the sincere and utmost regards of your devoted servant

P. Tchaikovsky

Address. Moscow. Imperial Conservatory of music

'THEIR SOUND IS NOT UNLIKE A FAST DRILL ON A REAR MOLAR'

THE RAMONES: MUSICIANS, DEGENERATES OR DENTISTS

The origin of punk rock is a subject of hot debate. Though many have attempted to identify the flashpoint of the provocative genre, there remains a lack of consensus on which act can be credited as *the* progenitors of punk. In truth, and as is the case with all social phenomena, the flame of punk rock was ignited by many strikes of the flint, with several bands having made unique contributions to its development. The New York Dolls – the trashy, hedonistic lyrics; the Stooges – the anarchic sound and the outlandish performance; the Sex Pistols – the anti-establishment image. When it comes to the raw, hard-hitting three-chord buzz that would form the foundation of punk rock, however, plaudits can go to only one band: the Ramones.

The Ramones formed in the New York City neighbourhood of Forest Hills, Queens in 1974. They had been brought together by a love of classic acts (such as the Beach Boys, the Beatles and Buddy Holly) and a hatred for the overproduced pop, rock and disco that then dominated the charts. Their music aimed to do one thing: smash the status quo of pop music conventions and bring rock 'n' roll back to its roots. In place of 14-minute songs with seven-minute solos came songs averaging two minutes or less; in place of melodic funky disco tunes – cold, hard, unadulterated rock 'n' roll.

The fledgling band swiftly managed to carve out a reputation for themselves in the New York club scene for their hard-and-fast playing and chaotic performances. In just a year they had taken what they could from the city, and it was time, they decided, for the next step in their career. It was time to let America know who the Ramones were and what they stood for.

The press release that was launched upon the American media was unpolished and erratic. It featured handwritten notes scrawled in the margins, and told the story of who the Ramones were on and off the stage.

Though the band struggled to achieve commercial success in their own right, they have since come to be known as one of the most influential rock bands of all time, and they were inducted into the Rock & Roll Hall of Fame in 2002. Even today, with all the original band members now deceased, their molar-rattling sound continues to inspire the next generation of punk rock outfits the world over.

THE RAMONES, FROM LEFT TO RIGHT: DEE-DEE, TOMMY, JOEY AND JOHNNY, 1978

From the Ramones to the media, 1975

THE RAMONES *– that's a nice name – Sam* [handwritten]

The Ramones are not an oldies group, they are not a glitter group, they don't play boogie music and they don't play the blues. The Ramones are an original Rock and Roll group of 1975, and their songs are brief, to the point and every one a potential hit single.

The quartette [*sic*] consists of Johnny ^*oldest*, Joey ^*youngest*, Dee Dee ^*embarrassing*, and Tommy Ramone. Johnny, the guitarist, plays with such force that his sound has been compared to a hundred howitzers going off. Joey, the lead singer, is an arch villain whose lanky frame stands threatening center stage. Dee Dee is Bass guitar and the acknowledged handsome one of the group, and Tommy is the drummer whose pulsating playing launches the throbbing sound of the band.

The Ramones all originate from Forest Hills and kids who grew up there either became musicians, degenerates or dentists. The Ramones are a little of each. Their sound is not unlike a fast drill on a rear molar.

'I WANT PEOPLE TO HEAR MY VOICE AND JUST . . . FORGET THEIR TROUBLES FOR FIVE MINUTES'

AMY WINEHOUSE DREAMS OF BEING A STAR
With her debut and sophomore albums *Frank* (2003) and *Back to Black* (2006), Amy Winehouse sent shockwaves through the British pop scene. By blending such genres as soul, blues, funk and jazz, Winehouse (1983–2011) successfully produced a neo-soul sound that was simultaneously rooted in a rich tapestry of musical inspiration and also wholly new and unmistakably unique to her.

Of course, what was so fundamental to the creation of this distinctive sound was Winehouse's rich contralto voice. As is typified by the iconic tracks 'Rehab' and 'Back to Black', her voice not only bound together the various genres from which she drew, but also formed the powerhouse of her sound, instilling her music with a quality that has since led her to be regarded as one of the finest singers of the new millennium.

Amy Winehouse was forever the creative. As an impulsive and boisterous child she drew little pleasure from formalized education, and her school years were marked by frequent trips to the headmistress's office. Winehouse's seemingly boundless energy demanded an artistic channel, and in music she found such an outlet. Music had been ever-present in the home while she was growing up, and when the time came to choose a secondary school, Winehouse was adamant it needed to be one that could accommodate her growing passion for musical performance.

In the end she settled on the Sylvia Young Theatre School, an institution that boasts an impressive roster of alumni including Keeley Hawes, Billie Piper and Dua Lipa. Initially, Winehouse's parents were opposed to the idea, believing it was in her best interests to attend a traditional secondary school before going on to a theatre school. In typical Amy Winehouse fashion, however, she applied anyway without their knowing, and penned this letter as part of her application explaining the reasons why she was committed to pursuing a life in music.

Much to Winehouse's delight (and the surprise of her parents) she was offered an audition at the prestigious school, for which she sang Frank Sinatra's 'The Sunny Side of the Street'. Unsurprisingly, the panel were blown away by her performance, and offered her a scholarship which served as the launchpad for her subsequent career.

AMY WINEHOUSE

From Amy Winehouse to the admissions board of the Sylvia Young Theatre School, 1995

SYLVIA YOUNG THEATRE SCHOOL

WRITTEN ASSESSMENT

Name: <u>Amy Winehouse</u> School Year Group: <u>8</u>

All my life I have been loud, to the point of being told to shut up. The only reason I have to be this loud is because I ha you have to scream to be heard in my family. My family? Yes, you read it right. My mum's side is perfectly fine, apart from my demon grandmother, but my dad's family are the singing, dancing, all nutty musical extravaganza. I've been told I was gifted with a lovely voice, and

I guess my dad's to blame for that. Although unlike my dad + his background + ancestors, I want to do something with these talents I've been 'blessed' with. My dad is content to sing loudly in his office, and sell windows.

My mother, however, is a chemist. She is quiet, reserved, sometimes goes mad and was the main contributor to my looks.

I would say that my school life and school reports are filled with 'could do better's', and 'doesn't work to her full potential'. This is because my present school is a horrible place to go to every day. But I guess all schools are.

I want to go somewhere where I am stretched right to my limits and perhaps even beyond. To singin [sic] in lessons without being told to shut up (provided they <u>are</u> singing lessons). But mostly, I have this dream to be very famous. To work on stage. It's a life-long ambition. I want people to hear my voice and just . . . forget their troubles for five minutes. I want to be remembered for being an actress, a singer, for sell-out concerts and sell-out West-End and Broadways shows. For being just . . . me.

CHAPTER TWO

INSPIRATION

The word 'inspire' derives from the Latin *inspirare* – to *breathe into*. It is a word with deeply supernatural connotations, and there is a long tradition of artists, and perhaps especially composers, believing themselves to be inspired – *breathed into* – by God or some other higher power. This can be taken to extremes, of course. A pervasive myth perpetuated by those whose interests lie in selling associated tourist tat in Vienna and Salzburg is that Mozart was a 'conduit' for the voice of God. Peter Shaffer played on and turbocharged this myth to great effect in his 1979 play (and the subsequent film of 1984), *Amadeus*, for which those hawkers of the ubiquitous marzipan balls are, one imagines, eternally grateful. There is no evidence that Mozart thought of himself as God's conduit, but there is *something* about outrageous talent such as Mozart's – talent so far beyond the ordinary – that leaves both those exposed to it and those who possess it reaching for the language of the divine.

Along with God, landscapes have long triggered the artistic impulse, and the landscape of Gloucestershire in particular sits at the heart of an entire British musical movement. Within that landscape, rising above the village of Churchdown between Cheltenham and Gloucester, sits Chosen Hill – a topographical feature that has provided more than its fair share of inspiration to composers of the so-called 'English revival'. Gerald Finzi stood atop the hill on New Year's Eve 1925, listening to the sound of bells rising from the valley below, and thus was conceived his wonderful *In Terra Pax*. But it is another English composer, a few years earlier, whose words we read in this chapter musing on Chosen Hill and the nature of writing music 'depicting' a place (something we revisit later in this volume in the chapter entitled 'The Space Between the Notes'). Herbert Howells is a composer whose reputation, while never entirely overlooked, has continued to grow in the half-century since his death. His was not a particularly happy life, and it is often advanced that his finest works tend to be responses to profound trauma: the *Elegy* (inscribed to the memory of his fellow RCM student Frances Purcell Warren, killed in the Great War) and his masterpiece, *Hymnus paradisi*, written in the wake of the death of his nine-year-old son from polio in 1935, being the best examples. But the elegiac, nostalgic impulse in his music is apparent before these appalling events, including in two works of around this time inspired by Chosen Hill: the A minor Piano Quartet and the miniature 'The Chosen Tune', dedicated to the woman who would become his wife: 'Perhaps the presence of a certain person is not entirely unrelated to the frame-of-mind which the Hill produces in me . . .'

So is it really 'landscape' inspiring Howells, or is it in fact 'love'? The answer of course is that it is a potent combination of the two – and presumably of many more factors combining, just as did those equally nebulous ingredients of 'greatness' discussed some pages ago. But let us add 'love' to the list so far comprised of 'God' and 'landscape' as common sources of inspiration to artists, composers and musicians included. Love is shot through this chapter: romantic love as seen with Leoš Janáček; *philia* as demonstrated by Elgar, Teresa Carreño and others; and, in the case of Richard Wagner, a splendidly unsubtle bit of self-love.

There is perhaps a tendency to look at 'the greats' and forget that behind the talent which mixes with inspiration (from wherever it derives) to produce, just occasionally, an enduring work of art, lie thousands of hours of hard work: hours of scales, compositional exercises and practice that have often begun at an unbelievably young age. The idea of Mozart as a mere conduit for God is not only wrong but also an appalling slight on Mozart himself: God might inspire and He might even bestow the seed of talent, but the creative process and the cultivation of that talent are hard and costly, as these letters prove.

'IN HIS FIRST FIRE HE WAS BRILLIANT; BUT THAT FIRE DIMINISHES EACH TIME HE STRIVES TO REKINDLE IT'

DRAWING DRY THE WELLSPRING OF INSPIRATION: JEAN-PHILIPPE RAMEAU REFLECTS

In 1722, the French composer Jean-Philippe Rameau published a work that transformed how the learned circles of Europe perceived the art of music. The work was titled *Traité de l'harmonie réduite à ses principes naturels* (Treatise on Harmony Reduced to Its Natural Principles), and in it Rameau (1683–1764) argued that music is to be understood first and foremost as a science. To compose music, therefore, is to perform a mathematical equation akin to those which determine the shape of the world and the wider universe.

Rameau's work captures the zeitgeist of the Enlightenment philosophy sweeping across Europe in the eighteenth century. Indeed, the work earned him the epithet 'the Isaac Newton of music', and made him one of the most influential music theorists of the Baroque Age. A further label Rameau's theories earned him was that of a 'learned' musician, though this was a title he was eager to distance himself from.

At a time when emotive conceptions of music were the prevailing mode of thought, to be known as an objective musician could be highly damaging to a composer's career, and Rameau found he had to repeatedly allay the concerns of potential employers and collaborators who feared his pieces might lack the passion of a more emotionally driven composer. One such instance occurred in 1727, five years after the publication of his treaty, when he wrote to the French author Antoine Houdar de la Motte. Rameau was eager to break into the world of opera, and he contacted la Motte in the hope of commissioning a libretto to which he could compose.

In an effort to relieve the author of any doubts as to his abilities, Rameau weighed up the pros and cons of science versus nature in the art of music. Ultimately, he posited, it is a question of whether one follows one's head or one's heart. If the latter, then a composer must be aware that they are drawing from a finite resource, for while inspiration from the soul can burn brightly, it is also soon exhausted. Moreover, it was Rameau's belief that one who composes from the heart limits themselves to music indicative only of their own character. Conversely, following one's head is a sure way for a composer to safeguard their longevity. Certainly to adhere dogmatically to the rules of composition runs the risk of producing sterile music devoid of emotion, intuition and character. Equally, however, it is within these structures and principles that a composer can explore a diverse array of sounds, and channel a platitude of emotions.

PORTRAIT OF JEAN-PHILLIPPE RAMEAU PAINTED BY
JACQUES-ANDRE-JOSEPH AVED, C. 1728

From Jean-Philippe Rameau to Antoine Houdar de la Motte of the Académie Royale de Musique, 1727

Paris, 25 October 1727

. . . Whatever reasons you may have, Sir, for apprehending that my music for the stage will not be greeted so favourably as that of a composer apparently more experienced in that style of music, permit me to contest them and at the same time to justify the prejudice I feel in my own favour, without claiming to derive from my learning any advantages other than those which you too will feel to be legitimate. Those who speak of 'a learned musician' ordinarily mean a man conversant with all aspects of the different combination of notes; but at the same time he is believed to be so absorbed in those combinations that to them he sacrifices everything – sentiment, common sense, wit and reason. Such a man is merely an academic musician, of an academy concerned with notes and nothing more; so that people do well to prefer to him the musician who sets less store by his erudition than by his taste. The latter, however, whose taste has been formed solely by comparisons within his own range of feeling, cannot excel in more than a few styles at most – I mean, in those related to his temperament. Is he naturally tender? Then he will well express tenderness; is his character quick, playful, frivolous, etc.? His music will be correspondingly so; but let him depart from these characteristics which are his by nature, and you will no longer recognize him. Moreover, since he draws everything from his imagination, with no help from art, by his recourse to various expressions, he at last wears himself out. In his first fire he was brilliant; but that fire diminishes each time he strives to rekindle it, and he ends by offering us nothing but repetitions and platitudes . . .

Nature has not entirely withheld her gifts from me, and I have not devoted myself to forming combinations of notes so far as to forget their intimate connection with natural beauty, which by itself is sufficient to please, but which is not easily found in a soil which lacks seed and above all, which has made its last efforts . . .

You need only come to hear from yourself what character I have bestowed upon the *Sauvages*, which appeared in the *Théâtre Italien* a year or two ago, and how I interpreted such titles as *Les Soupirs*, *Les Tendres Plaintes*, *Les Cyclopes*, *Les Tourbillons* (these being the swirls of dust stirred up by high winds), *L'Entretien des Muses*, a *Musette*, a *Tambourin*, etc.; you will not appear to make a great display of learning in my productions, where I strive to employ the art that conceals arts; for in them I consider only people of taste, and learned men not at all, since there are many of the former and scarce any of the latter sort . . .

Here at least you have matter enough for reflection . . .

'I FEEL THAT IN EVERY FRESH PIECE I SUCCEED BETTER IN LEARNING TO WRITE EXACTLY WHAT IS IN MY HEART, AND AFTER ALL THAT IS THE ONLY RIGHT RULE I KNOW'

FELIX MENDELSSOHN'S DEVOTION TO COMPOSING MUSIC FROM THE SOUL

The Romantic composer Jakob Ludwig Felix Mendelssohn Bartholdy, known more commonly as Felix Mendelssohn (1809–47), never seemed short of inspiration. Even by the tender age of 12, Mendelssohn had written as many symphonies as years he had lived, as well as four operas and numerous chamber and piano pieces.

In terms of his style, he drew heavily from the work of earlier composers he admired, such as Bach, Handel, Carl Maria von Weber and, most notably, Beethoven. As for the substance of his compositions, Mendelssohn derived inspiration from a variety of sources. From theatre, William Shakespeare's *A Midsummer Night's Dream* for his accompanying Op. 61 (most famous today for producing the world-famous 'Wedding March'). From poetry, the works of his close friend Johann Wolfgang von Goethe served as the basis for the overture *Meeresstille und glückliche Fahrt* ('Calm Sea and Prosperous Voyage', Op. 27, 1828), and the cantata *Die erste Walpurgisnacht* ('The First Walpurgis Night', Op. 60, 1832). From the natural world, Mendelssohn's time travelling Europe provided the impetus for his

Italian and Scottish symphonies, as well as the famous overture, *The Hebrides*. Beyond all these influences, Mendelssohn knew he could always rely on himself to be the root of his inspirations. It was for him and him alone that he produced his music, and he was determined to remain true to this conviction, regardless of public opinion.

Such was the position Mendelssohn communicated in this letter to fellow musician and close friend, Ferdinand David. David had become the concertmaster at the Gewandhaus Orchestra in 1835, a position where he worked closely with Mendelssohn, and in this letter Mendelssohn congratulated David on his progression as a musician. In so doing, Mendelssohn also gives an update on his own compositions, and it is clear his head is bursting full of ideas. One such piece – 'the one in E minor' – would come to be one of his most famous works, Op. 64 Violin Concerto.

PORTRAIT OF FELIX MENDELSSOHN BY CARL JAEGER

From Felix Mendelssohn to Ferdinand David, 1838

Berlin, July 30th, 1838.

Dear David,

Many thanks for your letter, which gave me great pleasure. Since I came here I have been constantly thinking how really delightful it is that we are to meet and live together, instead of your being in one place and I in another, following our avocations without hearing much of each other, which is, no doubt, the case with many good fellows in our dear yet rather aggravating Fatherland; but on reflecting further, I discovered that there are not many musicians who, like yourself, pursue steadily the broad straight road in art, or in whose active course I could feel the same intense delight that I do in yours. Such things are seldom said in conversation, therefore let me write to-day, how much your rapid and welcome development during the last few years has surprised and rejoiced me; it is often grievous to me to see so many with the noblest aspirations, but inferior talents, and others with great talents yet low tendencies; so that to see true genius, combined with right good will, is doubly cheering. People of the former class swarm here; almost all the young musicians who visit me may, with few exceptions, be included in that number. They praise and prize Gluck and Handel, and all that is good, and talk about them perpetually, and yet what they do is an utter failure, and so very tedious . . .

No doubt, you are preparing many new things for next winter, and I rejoice heartily in the idea of hearing them. I have just finished my third quartet in D major, and like it much. May it only please you as well! — I almost think it will, for it is more spirited, and seems to me likely to be more grateful to the players than the others. I intend in a few days to begin to write out my symphony, and to complete it in a short time, probably while I am still here. I should also like to write a violin concerto for you next winter. One in E minor runs in my head, the beginning of which gives me no peace. My symphony shall certainly be as good as I can make it, but whether it will be popular and played on the barrel-organs, I cannot tell. I feel that in every fresh piece I succeed better in learning to write exactly what is in my heart, and after all that is the only right rule I know. If I am not adapted for popularity, I will not try to acquire it, nor seek after it; and if you think this wrong, then I ought rather to say I *cannot* seek after it, for really I *cannot*, but would not if I could. What proceeds from within, makes me glad in its outward workings also, and therefore it would be very gratifying to me were I able to fulfil the wish you and my friends express; but I can do nothing towards it or about it. So much in my path has fallen to my share without my having even once thought of it, and without any effort on my part, that perhaps it may be the case with this also; if not, I shall not grumble on the subject, but console myself by knowing that I did what I could, according to my best powers and my best judgement. I have *your* sympathy, and *your* delight in my works, and also that of some valued friends. More could scarcely be desired. A thousand thanks, then, for your kind expressions and for all your friendship towards me. —Your

Felix M.B.

'MY SOLE REASON FOR LIVING IS THE WONDEROUS LOVE WHICH DESCENDS UPON ME LIKE DROPS OF DEW FROM THE HEART OF MY ROYAL FRIEND – AS THOUGH FROM THE LAP OF GOD – FRUCTIFYING NEW SEEDS OF LIFE WITHIN ME!'

RICHARD WAGNER AND THE SWAN KING

The start of 1864 marked a low point in the career of Richard Wagner (1813–83). He had just spent the last 12 years in exile following his involvement as a minor revolutionary in the unsuccessful Dresden May Uprising of 1848, and though he had now been granted permission to re-enter Germany, his years abroad in France and Austria had left him penniless. Life as a fugitive in the

metropolitan capitals of Europe had not been cheap, and Wagner's
financial difficulties were exacerbated by the debts he had accrued
prior to his exile that now returned to haunt him. In fact, there
seemed little hope of reprieve for the struggling composer. That
is, until Ludwig II, King of Bavaria, requested an audience with
Wagner on 4 May 1864.

Ludwig had come to the throne of Bavaria that same year aged only
18. He had been a devoted admirer of Wagner ever since hearing
Lohengrin at the age of 15, and one of his first acts as king was to
offer a lifeline to his idol. Ludwig unbridled Wagner of his financial
troubles by settling all of his accounts, and provided him with lavish
accommodation near his royal castle of Hohenschwangau.

Wagner found Ludwig's patronage immensely reinvigorating, and
he set about working on his compositions with a renewed energy.
One of the first projects he returned to was the now world famous
operatic epic *Der Ring des Nibelungen*. He had begun composing the
first part of the opera in 1848 at the time of his exile, and by 1864
had reached the third part of the cycle, entitled *Siegfried*. Writing
to Ludwig on the progress of the opera, Wagner revelled in the
composition of act 3 of scene 1 which centres on the mysterious
figure of the all-father, Wotan.

The fawning tone of the letter reflects Wagner's aim of stroking
the ego of his royal patron to secure his continued support. As
Wagner would soon find out, however, Ludwig needed little
encouragement in this regard; in fact, his enthusiasm would prove
at times to be overwhelming. So eager was he to have Wagner's
work performed, for instance, that Ludwig forced the composer
to stage the first two parts of *Der Ring* at the National Theatre in
Munich in 1870, despite his desire to wait until the entire cycle
was complete and have a bespoke purpose-built venue constructed.
Thankfully for Wagner, he managed to realize his dream in 1876
when (with the reluctant financial backing of Ludwig) he had
the epic performed in its entirety at the specially built Bayreuth
Festspielhaus.

WILHELM RICHARD WAGNER, 1871

From Richard Wagner to King Ludwig II of Bavaria, 1864

Munich, 6 November 1864

My glorious and dearly beloved King,

There is a secret which can be revealed to my august and gracious friend only in the hour of my death: but then it will become clear to him what today must seem obscure — that *he* alone is the creator and author of all that the world will attribute to my name from this day on. My sole reason for living is the wonderous love which descends upon me like drops of dew from the heart of my royal friend — as though from the lap of God — fructifying new seeds of life within me! Last All Souls' Day I felt as though I were garlanding my own tomb with the gladsome flowers of this love. In truth, I – am no more! I have endured and suffered too much; life and its increasingly alien aspects have drawn me away for ever from my own inner self towards a state of dissipation which has finally grown too deep for me, and too disturbing. Now that I can finally compose my thoughts once more, – and only the magic power of your love and inspiration has made this possible, – I feel as though I am beginning a new and second life upon the grave of my old existence! And the sole creator of this life is my gracious friend, the saviour who leads me to a new religion, a religion which brings forth a second, new life from deep within me, – a life which knows not a death! –

It is to my royal friend that I dedicate the convalescent's new-found strength in these feeble lines herewith. I may well hope that, as a result of the painful crisis which followed upon an earlier chronic illness, this selfsame [sic] illness will now be less afflicting than it has been previously, and that it may indeed be allayed for some time to come; so that I regard it as a good sign that, at the very moment of actually moving into my final refuge, I may look forward to the comforting prospect of an improvement in my health as well. Soon, indeed, very shortly, I shall be back at my work again, like a man reborn, and I shall not forsake it again until it is completely finished. It is a marvellous passage where I now have to resume composition, having put the finishing touches to a number of earlier passages! It is the most sublime of all scenes for the most tragic of all my heroes, Wotan, who is the all-powerful will-to-exist and who is resolved upon his own self-sacrifice; greater now in renunciation than he ever was when he coveted power, he now feels all-mighty, as he calls out to the earth's primeval wisdom, to Erda, the mother of nature, who had once taught him to fear for his end, telling her that dismay can no longer hold him in thrall since he now wills his own end with that selfsame [sic] will with which he had once desired to live. His end? He knows what Erda's primeval wisdom does not know: that he lives on in *Siegfried*. Wotan lives on in Siegfried as the artist lives on in his work of art: the freer and the more autonomous the latter's spontaneous existence and the less trace it bears of the creative artist – so that through it (the work of art), the artist himself is forgotten, – the more perfectly satisfied does the artist himself feel: and so, in a certain higher sense, *his* being forgotten, his disappearance, his death is – the life of the work of art. – This is the frame of mind in which I am now turning once again to the completion of my work: I want to be destroyed by my Siegfried – in order to live for ever! O beauteous death! –

With what awesome solemnity shall I now awaken *Brünnhilde* from her long sleep! She slept while Siegfried grew to young manhood. How significant this must all now seem to me! The last music I wrote was the woodbird's announcement to Siegfried that he would be able to waken Brünnhilde if he had not learnt the meaning of fear: laughing, he ran after the bird which, fluttering away, showed him the way to the magic rock. – This road, my gracious, royal friend! – this road was long and arduous for me. I believe I should never, never reach the rock. But if I am Wotan, I have now succeeded through Siegfried: it is *he* who awakens the maid, the most precious thing in the world. My work of art will live, - it lives! – . . .

'THE VARIATIONS HAVE AMUSED ME BECAUSE I'VE LABELLED 'EM WITH THE NICKNAMES OF MY PARTICULAR FRIENDS – YOU ARE NIMROD'

EDWARD ELGAR FINDS INSPIRATION CLOSE TO HOME

For many in Britain today, Edward Elgar's 'Nimrod' Variation is synonymous with the Remembrance Sunday commemorations held on 11 November every year to mark the end of the First World War. The slow swell of the melody into a dramatic climax makes for an immensely moving piece and fittingly captures the sombre reverence of the day. So too has its solemn sound made it a popular choice for events of national significance, as seen at the London Olympic Games opening ceremony in 2012. It is perhaps surprising, then, that this tear-jerking piece has its roots in a heartwarming tale of enduring friendship.

Nimrod forms one of the 14 variations included in what is commonly known as the *Enigma Variations* composed by Elgar between 1898 and 1899. Each of the variations was inspired by one of Elgar's friends, influences reflected in the dedication which read, 'To my friends pictured within'. Such figures included his wife Caroline, fellow musicians, Oxford dons, pupils and architects, and the inspirations stemmed from Elgar's close personal observations of these individuals' traits, quirks and habits – even their styles of speech.

In the case of 'Nimrod' – the ninth of the variations – the subject of Elgar's inspiration was his close friend and publisher, August Jaeger. While their relationship had begun as one of purely business, the two quickly developed a deep fondness for one another, and Jaeger grew to become an important advisor for Elgar. Such was the intimacy of their friendship that in the introduction to their collected letters, Jaeger is referred to as the 'godfather of Elgar's compositions'. Furthermore, the tenderness of their friendship is eminently noticeable in the casual tone of this letter in which Elgar informed Jaeger that he was one of the subjects of his compositions.

Concerning the name of the variation, Elgar drew on the name of the warrior hunter named in the book of Genesis to make a subtle linguistic pun relating to Jaeger's German nationality, with *Jäger* being the German word for 'hunter'. As to the composition of the piece, it is reported that Elgar here sought to dramatize a fateful moment when Jaeger lambasted him for suggesting he forsake a career in music. During this episode, Jaeger had drawn on the troubled experiences of his countryman, Beethoven, to emphasise his point, something which Elgar pays homage to in the style of the variation.

The piece, therefore, with its undulating yet progressive rise, is one of rebirth and redemption that distils Elgar's gratitude towards his old friend for convincing him to persevere in his efforts to become a composer.

THE COMPOSER EDWARD ELGAR

From Edward Elgar to August Jaeger, 1898

24th October 1898

My dear Jaeger,

Here is the 'Grecian ghost which unburied remains inglorious on the plain' or on the hills.

I hope the house-hunting is over satisfactorily and that you have peaceful prospects. Let me know.

Our woods look lovely but decidedly damp and rheumaticky — unromantic just now.

Since I've been back I have sketched a set of Variations (orkestra) [*sic*] on an original theme: the Variations have amused me because I've labelled 'em with the nicknames of my particular friends – you are Nimrod. That is to say I've written the variations each one to represent the mood of the 'party' – I've liked to imagine the 'party' writing the var: him (or her) self and have written what I think they w[oul]d. have written – if they were asses enough to compose – it's a quaint idea & the result is amusing to those behind the scenes & won't affect the hearer who 'nose nuffin'. What think you?

Much love & sunshine to you.

Ed. Elgar.

'DO YOU REALIZE THAT AS AN ARTIST I AM YOUR CREATION? DO YOU KNOW <u>HOW NECESSARY</u> YOU ARE TO ME AS AN ARTIST!'

TERESA CARREÑO PLEADS WITH HER MENTOR TO CONTINUE LIVING

Venezuelan pianist, composer and conductor Teresa Carreño was so startingly brilliant that she was often referred to as the 'Valkyrie of the Piano' – a grand title to live up to, though one hard earned. Carreño (1853–1917) cut her teeth on the grandest of stages, performing for the President of the United States, Abraham Lincoln, aged only nine, before embarking on a concert tour in Cuba; over 50 years later, Carreño returned to the White House to perform for President Woodrow Wilson in 1916. Despite reaching such dizzying heights at such a young age, Carreño never lost sight of her origins, or those individuals who had helped her grow into the remarkable musician she became.

Regina 'Ginka' Watson – Carreño's teacher, friend and mentor – was one such individual. Watson was herself an accomplished performer and composer, having trained with Franz Liszt and his pupil Karl Tausig, and Carreño had come under her tutelage in 1862, following the family's move to the United States. A close bond soon flourished between the two musicians, and Carreño never forgot the debt she owed to her old teacher, with the pair corresponding decades after their tutelage ended.

Following the loss of her husband, Watson wrote to her former pupil of the despair and disillusionment with life she now felt. In an effort to comfort her friend, Carreño wrote this letter in response, outlining the reasons her mentor had to keep on living. Not least was Carreño's desire for Watson to continue to guide her growth as a musician.

TERESA CARREÑO AT HER PIANO, C. 1915—17

From Teresa Carreño to Regina 'Ginka' Watson, 1913

January 5th 1913

My own beloved, my precious darling!

. . . I beg you on my knees, to live for us all, for all the friends who love you so tenderly so deeply. For my sake my Ginka, for my <u>artistic self</u>, for <u>my art</u>!

Do you realize that as an artist I am your creation? Do you know <u>how necessary</u> you are to me as an artist! You, my darling Beloved, have brought me to be what the world says I am. Through you I have had the courage to work and go on living, at times when <u>I was in despair</u> and did not care to live any longer. Not even the thought of my children gave me the energy which the thought of giving you a sorrow brought to one and made me go on living, go on in my profession. Do you know what would happen to me if you left me? Have you ever given this possibility a thought my darling? Well darling, the artist in me, would <u>die with you</u>. All my ambition of keeping myself, keeping alive my better self, which is my artistic self would disappear from the moment that I cannot have you as my guiding star, as my good angel in life. What ever I have accomplished, has been for <u>your sake</u> more than for mine, and without you my better self does not, <u>cannot exist</u>. And how much you have accomplished with one and <u>for me</u>, my beloved precious darling! Had it been possible for you to have been present at the banquet which was given to me at the Kaiserhof <u>here in Berlin</u>, where there was a gathering of so many of the great lights in our profession and been a witness of the great honor which they all paid me! And all this, <u>your work</u> my Ginka!! My thoughts went continually to you and to the time when you took me by the hand and gave me the courage, the strength and the means to come here and try and make myself a position and a name in Germany, which meant a name as an artist in the entire musical world. If you had seen the crowning of <u>your work</u>, I know that you would have felt a great satisfaction as an artist and as my <u>dearest</u> and <u>best</u> friend!

My darling, my beloved, you must not kill <u>me</u> as an artist, kill my better self, by taking your precious life. Wait my beloved, until I have finished my work. There is much for me to do yet and if you are not there, it will remain undone.

Goodbye for to-day my precious one. My heart is so full, that I cannot say any more to-day.

God bless you, God be with you and Help you find the strength to live for me and for all those whose happiness <u>you are</u>, my darling precious Ginka!

Your own

Teresa

Arthur and the children send you their heart tenderest love.

for a line from you, for a sign of life after the long long months of silence on your part. Thank you, my precious belovèd, for the the dear dad letter, and for remembering my birthday. It was just like you, my finka, not to forget your parents on that day and how it touched me. I ought to be used to all the tender loving actions of your great big heart; and yet, every time a new proof of it comes, it touches me as deeply and fills me with the utmost gratitude and makes me oh! so happy, my Belovèd!

No one better than I can understand your sorrow, your despair, for was I not, for long years, the witness of your happiness? Years of the most perfect happiness that this life contains were the years of your happy married life. It was our belovèd Lewie!

And yet my belovèd precious one, I beg you on my knees, to live for us all, for all the friends who love you so tenderly, so deeply, for my sake, my finka, for my artistic self, for my Art!

Do you realize that as an artist, I am your creation? Do you know how necessary you are to me as an artist? For you, my darling Belovèd, have brought me to be what the world says I am. Through you, I have had the courage to work and go on living, at times when I was in despair, and

did not care to live any longer. Not even the thought of the children gave me the energy which the thought of finny you a sorrow brought to me and made me go on living, go on in my profession.

Do you know what would happen to me if you left me? Have you ever asked this possibly a thought my darling? Well darling, the artist in me, would die with you. All my ambitions of keeping myself, keeping my better self, which is my artistic self, would disappear from the moment that I cannot have you as my guiding star, as my good angel in life. Whatever I have accomplished has been for your sake, more than for mine, and without you, my better self does not, cannot exist. And how

much you have accomplished with me and for me, my Belovèd precious Darling! Had it been possible for you to have been present at the Banquet which was given to me at the Kaiserhof here in Berlin, where there was a gathering of so many of the great lights in our profession and been a witness of the great honor which they all paid me! And all this, your work my finka! My thoughts went continually to you and to the time when you took me by the hand and gave me the courage, the strength and

'THIS IS A SERIOUS LETTER, WHICH IS WHY I'VE CHOSEN THIS IMPOSING FORMAT'

ARTHUR HONEGGER MAKES HIS CASE FOR A MUSICAL CAREER IN PARIS

In 1915, the composer Arthur Honegger found himself at a crossroads in his life and career. After a brief spell of military service at the Swiss borders, Honegger (1892–1955) returned to his studies at the Conservatoire de Paris with a renewed vision: he would no longer be dedicating hours to violin lessons in the hope of becoming a virtuoso, but would instead pursue the career of a composer.

Honegger had by no means been a child prodigy, but he realized that his sudden change of heart would come as a great surprise to his parents. Emboldened by the support of his teacher André Gédalge, Honegger wrote a 'serious' letter to his parents in which he laid out every conceivable counterargument to the protestations he expected them to make against his choice.

Honegger wrote with humility and confidence of his progress in harmony, counterpoint and fugue, underscoring his dedication to mastering the complexities of composition. Throughout the letter he grappled with the realities of pursuing this career, recognizing the long path ahead of him that was fraught with uncertainty – a tone perhaps taken to reassure his parents that he had considered the potential risks associated with his career choice, and one that many who defy their parents' expectations can relate to.

Honegger's letter provides a candid account of his evolving identity as a composer and serves as a testament to his enduring artistic vision. Moreover, it captures the essence of a young musician striking to carve out their place in the world.

ARTHUR HONEGGER POSES WITH A VIOLIN, C. 1910

From Arthur Honegger to his parents, 1915

28 April 1915

My dear parents,

This is a serious letter, which is why I've chosen this imposing format. To judge by Mama's suggestions about returning my books and music, and by what I remember of your remarks, you are thinking of this year as being the last I shall spend in Paris. After my military service I was to have gone to Germany to complete my studies. After much reflection, I have come to the conclusion that it would be far better to let me stay on next year in Paris, and I'll try and explain to you why.

I have now firmly chosen a career as a composer. I believe I have the natural disposition that is the principal basis for this, and so far all the musicians who have been competent to give an opinion have agreed in recognizing that I have a certain talent, which means that I may have a reasonable chance of getting somewhere. You probably have a vague idea of the difficulty of this career, since you know how many great composers have lived in humble obscurity all their lives and have made a success with the public only after their death. So, as the saying goes, my life will be 'a time of long patience' and I hope that you will have patience as well, that is to say, that you won't be discouraged if success seems to you to be long in coming.

Learning to be a composer is a long and time-consuming business. Even so, I believe I shall be able to complete my studies (I'm thinking of my academic studies, naturally, since one goes on learning all one's life), that is to say, that I'll know my craft, and after I leave Gédalge I shan't need any other teachers except the study of the great masters of all the ages. I'm working on fugue now and have practically finished everything to do with harmony and counterpoint. Next year I expect to finish studying fugue and to have enough knowledge of orchestration and what is called the study of composition to get by, and learn the rest from personal experience.

I think this is the place to say something about Gédalge's importance from the teaching point of view. Gédalge's *Treatise on Fugue* is the most complete work that has ever been written on the subject. It is used in conservatories all over Europe and all musicians agree that it's a masterpiece of clarity and logic. So I couldn't find anyone better than the author of this treatise to teach me fugue . . .

. . . From another point of view, when the war is over, it would be difficult for me to stay in Germany. I don't know the language well enough and my general outlook is too French for me to be welcome there. What's more, my musical sympathies with the new French school are growing daily. There's no doubting that, for the first time, France is currently at the head of musical developments. I got to know and love Reger and Strauss while I was in Switzerland, and I continue to love them, but I realized that composers such as Debussy, Dukas, d'Indy, Florent Schmitt and others were newer and more original and above all contained more feeling than the modern Germans. Strauss's music, considered on its own and apart from its orchestral clothing that is its principal strength (and a strength of genius in that composer), is infinitely less rich in invention than the music of Debussy, for example, and often contains things that are extremely banal and old-fashioned. Reger's music is admirably written, but it often lacks real imagination or emotion and for that reason constitutes an abuse of technical procedures . . .

'LAST SATURDAY MORNING I WALKED TO THE TOP AND LOOKED OUT ACROSS TO THE COUNTRY ROUND THE MALVERNS . . . FIVE MINUTES OF THAT VIEW WAS ENOUGH TO SET THE MUSICAL PART OF MY BRAIN GOING'

HERBERT HOWELLS DRAWS INSPIRATION FROM THE BEAUTY OF THE NATURAL WORLD
Among the lush green hills of rolling countryside nestled between the cities of Gloucester and Cheltenham lies Chosen Hill: a summit

of only 500ft, but which commands stunning views across the Severn Vale. It is, as the name suggests, as if the hill has been imbued with an exceptional, even divine quality, and it has served to inspire many a great artist who has witnessed the world from its peak. One was the English composer Herbert Howells, for whom the hill possessed a tangible spiritual allure.

Howells (1892–1983) became enamoured with Chosen Hill when studying as a pupil of the organist Herbert Brewer at Gloucester Cathedral, where he would while away his free time exploring the hill's various paths and beauty spots with his friend, the future poet Ivor Gurney. These experiences made an indelible mark on the young composer, and his fondness for the hill endured long after he left Gloucester for London in 1912 to study music at the Royal College of Music. Indeed, the hill served as the inspiration for his first mature composition, Piano Quartet in A minor (Op. 21), composed in 1916 and dedicated to 'the Hill at Chosen and Ivor Gurney who knows it'.

In a letter written to his brother soon after completing the piece, Howells reflected on the peculiar way in which he managed to translate the experience of this natural landscape into a musical composition. Even for him, the creator, it was a mysterious cognitive process, but there is no doubt the composition *was,* in his eyes at least, the hill in musical form.

That Howells had any energy at all to compose the piece is itself a wonder, for only a year earlier he had been diagnosed with Graves' disease, an autoimmune disorder affecting the thyroid, and given six months to live. Somehow, however, in among endless trips to London for treatment that involved injections of radium in his neck, Howells managed to continue composing, and the quartet was eventually published in 1918.

Thankfully, Howells managed to overcome his illness, and in the years that followed Chosen Hill continued to stimulate his creativity, a notable example being his 1920 piece *The Chosen Tune*, composed for his wife Dorothy Dawe and performed at their wedding.

HERBERT HOWELLS WORKING ON A NEW MUSICAL SCORE, 1947

From Herbert Howells to his brother Leonard, 1917

Friday Jan 19th 1917

[note written vertically in the margin] In case you have not read it in the papers I am enclosing a cutting containing the speech made by Lord Rosebery at the unveiling of the Gladstone Memorial – It is a marvel of fitness of expression – and masterly in the manner of linking up aspects of 1850 and 1917.

My Dear Leonard John.

For 'Hobson's Choice' and the note which accompanied it, many thanks! What effect the former will have on my brutal corn I am as yet unable to tell. Whatever it does, you shall hear of it.

The good-humoured banter, in your note, about the Hill of Chosen, was pleasant. Perhaps the presence of a certain person is not entirely unrelated to the frame-of-mind which the Hill produces in me: but – and the hour decapitated me if I swear it falsely – the share of that relationship in it is small. For it is, in very fact, a lovely hill, of a very definite and impressive personality, and wondrously changeful withal. I believe I told you that I had written a purely musical work about it? And possibly you wonder how a feature in landscape can translate itself into musical terms, and be so expressed? The process in my mind was vague: I could not describe, or even discern it entirely. But certain I am, that now the work is done, it is for me a perfectly similar thing (save of course, in the means of expression), to the hill itself. You, or anybody else, would fail to say 'that music is Chosen Hill!', because I believe that 'programme' music (i.e. music which sets out definitely to describe a scene, or sequence of events) is successful only within the minds of its individual creators. Beethoven said that he always composed to a picture; but he strongly insisted that the same music could not produce the <u>same</u> picture in two or more separate minds . . . So it is with my work on Chosen. I listen to it and derive the same emotions that are engendered by my actual presence on the Hill itself: if you listened to the work you might think of anything but a Hill . . . you could hardly see the place, to any advantage, from the trains. That is all the more reason why you must see it properly and leisurely someday . . . Last Saturday morning I walked to the top of it, stood against that fine old Church, and looked out across to the country round the Malverns, and at the Malverns themselves. Five minutes of that view was enough to set the musical part of my brain going. I walked to 'Glengarriff' [sic] – and by 2.30 in the afternoon I had begun and finished an Anthem. I have bestowed it on Dr Hugh Allen, of Oxford, and no doubt he will have it sung in New College there, where he is Sub-Warden and Organist of the Chapel . . . So it is that Chosen affects me . . . Long ago, even when I was only about 10 years old, I remember being similarly impressed by a walk with Father to Viney Hill. My poor little brain tried to fashion sounds when I got home that day: but, of course, it lacked the power to do so.

I often wonder what might be the results if children who are artistically moved by things and events had the technique which would allow of their expressing their conceptions of things. It would add a new chapter to Art, I believe; since what they did would be almost wholly lacking in sophistication. And of Art minus sophistication we (who begin saying and doing thinks [sic] only when we have already become sophisticated) know next to nothing. Folk songs and Folk-Love come nearest to the absolutely simple art product. And these things stand in great peril of being spoilt by contact with persons who, being themselves so many masses of sophisticated bones, blood and tissue, ally sophistications of accomplishment with the simple accomplishments of unsophistication! I have been angered many times by this stupid sort of alliance in 'arrangements' of Folk-tunes. And I saw the same failure and incongruity in an attempt made by some writer to re-tell 'in his own way' an old superstition of Irish Folk-Love. Damn their stupidities!

. . . But of course, sophistication in Art can be beautiful to a very rare degree. If you could only hear some of Bach's Fugues, and some of the later String Quartets of Beethoven, and realise what loveliness can be in super-fine creatures of the kind! You no doubt have similar things in the works of some of the rarer Painters . . .

All my love to you all,

Your affectionate brother. Herbert.

'I HAVE THE GREAT WEAKNESS OF BEING ABLE TO WRITE ONLY WHEN MY PUPPET EXECUTIONERS ARE MOVING ON THE SCENE'

NO LIBRETTO, NO INSPIRATION: PUCCINI SUFFERS FROM WRITER'S BLOCK

Take any one of the great operas, and at its heart you will find the creative partnership of a composer and librettist. Of the two, it is most often the composer who receives the lion's share of public praise. For the operas *The Marriage of Figaro* and *Don Giovanni* it is for most Mozart, not Lorenzo Da Ponte, who is brought to mind. *For Der Rosenkavalier* it is Richard Strauss, less Hugo von Hofmannsthal, that is remembered.

While the composer may get the glory, however, it should not obscure the fact that the libretto stands as the fundamental component of any opera. Without a libretto there can be no opera, for it is from language that an opera is formed, as the composer produces music which moulds to the emotions and events of the narrative. The librettist is, then, the composer's muse, and it is on them which their creative output rests.

Nowhere is the scale of dependence made more apparent than in the letter written by Giacomo Puccini (1858–1924) to his librettist Giuseppe Adami. The two had been introduced by Puccini's publisher, Giulio Ricordi, in 1912, who recommended Adami as a possible candidate to work on one of Puccini's projects that would eventually become the comedic opera *La Rondine*, which premiered in 1917.

According to many of his biographers, Puccini could often be a challenging individual to work with; in Adami he found an eager collaborator whose more reserved disposition lent itself to a balanced and fruitful working partnership. No collaboration is without its challenges, however, and the pair did occasionally come to blows, perhaps most notably in 1920 when Puccini was working on an opera that would become his magnum opus.

With its roots in an epic poem dating back to the twelfth century, the story of Turandot instantly enchanted Puccini, who saw a great opportunity to stage the tale of daring adventure and love as an opera for the first time. Such was his enthusiasm that he found every moment without a libretto agony, and within weeks of deciding to produce the opera was lambasting his usual collaborator to push him into action.

The healthy amount of emotional blackmail in Puccini's letters to Adami eventually had its effect, and the two worked with another writer, Renato Simoni, to produce the opera. Unfortunately,

Puccini did not live to see the completion of his great project. His diligent collaborators continued in his honour, however, and *Turandot* premiered in 1926, two years after Puccini's death.

From Giacomo Puccini to Giuseppe Adami, 1920

17th, 11:20 P.M.

Dear Adamino,

If I touch the piano my hands get covered with dust. My desk is piled up with letters — there isn't a trace of music. Music? Useless if I have no libretto. I have the great weakness of being able to write only when my puppet executioners are moving on the scene. If only I could be a purely symphonic writer! I should then at least cheat time . . . and my public. But that was not for *me*. I was born so many years ago — oh, so many, too many, almost a century . . . and Almighty God touched me with his little finger and said: 'Write for the theatre — mind, only for the theatre.' And I have obeyed the supreme command. Had He marked me out for some other task perhaps I should not be, as now, without material. O you, who say you are working while you are really doing something quite different — films, plays, poetry, articles — and never think, as you ought to think, of one who has the earth under his feet and yet feels the ground receding from him every hour and every day as if a landslip would swallow him up! I get such nice encouraging letters, but if, instead of these, one act were to arrive of our glittering Princess, don't you think it would be better? You would give me back my calm and my confidence, and the dust would not settle on my piano any more, so much banging would I do, and my desk would have its brave array of scoring sheets again. O you of the city, think to more purpose of one who is waiting in the country! I need not only the first act, but the third also, since then Act II would be finished. And *La Rondine*? When are you bringing it to me? It is urgent because it has forty theatres waiting.

Affectionate regards to you and Renato.

'IF IT WEREN'T FOR YOU, FROM WHOM THE SPARKS FALL ON ME AND CATCH FIRE, I'D NOT BE WHAT I AM!'

LEOŠ JANÁČEK'S MUSE

Some musicians are lucky enough to find instant stardom, while others toil tirelessly for years for the same recognition. One such musician for whom the world took longer to wake up to his genius was Leoš Janáček (1854–1928). Though he embarked on a career in music in the late 1800s, Janáček's folk-influenced compositions never quite captured the attention of audiences in the Czech capital of Prague until a change of fortune in 1916 saw Janáček's opera *Jenůfa* finally performed in the Prague National Theatre. Janáček, now aged 61, finally found himself propelled into the international limelight.

The years that followed the success of *Jenůfa* saw a surge in Janáček's creative output as he produced many of his best-known works, including *Káťa Kabanová* (1921), *The Cunning Little Vixen* (1923), the *Sinfonietta* (1926), and the *Glagolitic Mass* (1926).

Like many of his contemporaries, Janáček drew inspiration from the events of his life – notably the tragic death of his daughter, to whose memory he dedicated *Jenůfa* – as well as the world around him, with Eastern European folk music and stories a major influence. The source for his later works, however, can be traced back to a chance meeting in 1917.

Often struggling with exhaustion, Janáček became a regular visitor to the Czech spa town Luhačovice. During a period of convalescence following his successes in Prague, Janáček visited the resort to take the restorative waters, and made the acquaintance of Kamila Stösslová, with whom he would be utterly infatuated from that moment until the end of his life. When they parted at the end of his stay, Janáček immediately initiated a correspondence with his new muse that would eventually total over 700 letters.

Janáček's intense passion for Stösslová was, however, entirely one-sided: not only was Kamila happily married (much to Janáček's dismay), but she was also 38 years his junior, and showed little enthusiasm for his ardent pursuit of her affection. Consequently, her letters in response were often muted, and she showed little curiosity in his work as a composer. The pleasantness of her otherwise rather plain correspondence was, however, enough to sustain the idealized image Janáček had created of her, and she was the reluctant protagonist in many of his great works – for instance, the main characters Káťa and Emilia Marty in the operas *Káťa Kabanová* and *The Makropulos Affair*.

In this letter written just a year before his death, Janáček showered his muse with affectionate praise for the ways she stimulated his creativity. Kamila, though unmoved by his advances, remained a dear correspondent and was with the composer when he died in 1928.

LEOŠ JANÁČEK, 1914

From Leoš Janáček to Kamila Stösslová, 1927

Brno, 14 December 1927

My dear Kamila

I was already thinking that the doctor would send me to the bed! A proper cold; I have to inhale camphor dissolved in alcohol and take some sort of pills, five of them daily, in which one can smell menthol.

Otherwise I'm well! The heart's good, kidneys clean. Anyone could take me for a sixty-year-old. Well I'm still fit for life – and, a little, for my lady, for my Kamila?

So back to work – excited by reminiscences!

Oh, there were so many of them! You'll have a burden with me! But after this warning that I could sometimes think ill of you – I'll tame myself after that warning! A single warning glance from you – and I'll become tame. There was a wild animal in me – I'll storm out my passion in music! And then they ask where does that youthfulness in my composition come from! If it weren't for you, from whom the sparks fall on me and catch fire, I'd not be what I am!

And now our attaché in Vienna, Mr Vavrečka, has invited me to talk about my work and method of composition in Vienna. He wants to invite a large gathering.

I'd have to say to them: 'my soul and feeling is warmed and comes to the boil only through a single woman – but you must understand that I cannot name her, nor even describe her to you!' And you could best tell them that: I'm at my writing-desk, I feel your foot on mine, I throw down my pen, I'd embrace you, and in a moment I scrawl on the paper. It seems even worse; as if the pen were fighting with something that can't be seen.

This is the reason: the notes would like to slide along the moist lips of my Kamila – and they have to sit on the paper!

That's why my compositions have become so wild.

And what about you now?

Describe everything to me nicely as usual, even tell who took you on the motorbike! But if you don't want to, I won't insist on it. Actually I don't even want to know. It's a shame to shade the sun when it's shining, and we both love it.

And Kamila, you're better off because for weeks you're just on your own, alone – better off than me, who steals moments for himself! You know what it is to get under someone's feet! It's only through my work that I [can] exact privacy and myself with you, while you can dream in comfort, in that fiery glow. I carry a heavy burden. You must help me. Tell me if there's something about Fibich and Anežka in the second book.

If I could put those kisses into a box like live butterflies – now I'd let them go and catch them, catch them!

Keep well!

Write lots, nicely and openly.

Yours for ever

L.

14 December (Wednesday) 1927 at night
Thus I finish my day – every day.

CHAPTER THREE

THE SPACE BETWEEN THE NOTES

'There is so much talk about music, and yet so little really said,' writes Mendelssohn from Berlin in October 1842. Not, perhaps, an observation to which attention should be drawn in a book of letters about music; still less in a passage of writing introducing a chapter of those letters. But Mendelssohn is right, of course. One could read all the millions upon millions of words written throughout history about, say, Beethoven, but would that result in *understanding*? Would one *understand* Beethoven if one had just read about, never *heard*, those first two chords of the Third Symphony which herald the arrival (to some, at least) of the Romantic period? Or never *felt* the hammering of fate on the door of their soul at the outset of the Fifth Symphony? Or never been carried along by the rippling, unsettling arpeggios of the first movement of the piano sonata which later came to be known as the 'Moonlight'? Could one simply *read about* the late quartets – those extraordinary, exquisite works that flowed from the silent prison of Beethoven's deafness about which Schubert reportedly wrote, 'After this, what is left for us to write?' – and hope to comprehend them?

There is a lot of evidence for the existence of music. There are scores, but they are paper and ink. There are CDs, but they are plastic and booklet inserts. There are concert halls, but they are bricks and mortar. The only way we can be absolutely sure that music exists is by *experiencing* it: by listening to it or performing it. Asked to explain it or define it, most of us could make a reasonable attempt at discussing sound waves and frequencies and perhaps go into detail about melody and harmony and rhythm and timbre and metre. But we all know, fundamentally, in our hearts, that it's about more than these things; that our explanations can only go so far in conveying this extraordinary art form – this phenomenon – which drives people to dedicate their lives to its performance and to its study. '[Music] is the Queen of the senses,' writes Cassiodorus in his fifth-century letter attempting to source a new harpist for the king of France; 'when she comes forth from her secret abiding place all other thoughts are cast out.'

The title of this chapter is drawn from a quotation attributed to the poet and civil rights activist Maya Angelou: 'Music was my refuge. I could crawl into the space between the notes and curl my back to loneliness.' It's a powerful idea, and one that emanates from the same place in the soul as Cassiodorus's sentiment: some music will banish – briefly – the temporal preoccupations of the king of France just as it will alleviate – briefly – Maya Angelou's loneliness. It distracts and it consoles; it entertains and it edifies.

But there is a danger here, and it is one upon which Gustav Holst, in his letter of 1917, alights, albeit light-heartedly, when he observes that 'the average amateur's way of using music as a sedative or stimulant is purgatory and the professional way of using music as a topic of conversation or as a means of money getting is hell.' Where sedatives or stimulants are required – or desired – up grows an industry to supply them: it is no different when those sedatives or stimulants are musical rather than chemical. What results (according to some, at least) is the 'commodification' of music, one expression of which is the packaging up of excerpts of larger works to be prescribed and consumed when the listener requires stimulation, or indeed sedation. Thus we get radio programmes broadcast for an hour from 10 p.m. consisting only of chunks hacked off complete works designed to help the listener wind down from the day and fall asleep. The aural equivalent, then, of a generous glass of Pinot Grigio, not Hildegard's 'divine melody of praise which Adam, in company with the angels, enjoyed in God before his fall'.

Nestled alongside the commodification debate in the space between the notes is that other great extra-musical preoccupation: what a piece of music is *about*. Here, in a sense, we return to Mendelssohn, finding him of a mind with Hans Christian Andersen: 'where words fail, music speaks.' Nevertheless, a great many words have been dedicated to the question of whether music which does not set a text (i.e. instrumental music) can be *about* something, or rather can contain within it extra-musical meaning of a narrative or descriptive sort. The nature of music is such, of course, that it is impossible for two people to listen to the same piece and for it to spark an identical series of thoughts and associations – for the same image to be conjured in the eyes of the two listeners' minds. While a painter cannot dictate – although they may be able to strongly direct – the viewer of their painting's emotional response to it, they can at least be sure that if they paint a picture of a vase then the viewer's instant reaction will be, more often than not, to recognize a vase.

Franz Liszt, whose compositional output contains a number of perhaps the clearest-cut examples of music being *about* something (the 'symphonic poem'), gave a name to this phenomenon: 'programme music'. The 'programme' in question, he wrote, was 'a preface added to a piece of instrumental music, by means of which the composer intends to guard the listener against a wrong poetical interpretation, and to direct his attention to the poetical idea of the whole or to a particular part of it.' For the record, the 'opposite' of programme music came to be known as 'absolute music', which almost certainly does not exist: how could it, except if being played solely to robots? (Roger Scruton describes absolute music as 'not so much an agreed idea as an aesthetic problem'.)

Both Schoenberg and Mendelssohn have strong views about the 'programme' of their music. Schoenberg doesn't mind that Alma Mahler (whose husband Gustav had a notoriously difficult relationship with programmes, issuing them for his symphonies and then on more than one occasion withdrawing them) has a clear view of what his music is 'about', but refuses to accept that there is a 'right' interpretation. In fact, he goes further:

> I do not want to be understood – I want to express myself – but I hope I will be misunderstood. It would be terrible if people could see through me. For this reason I prefer to say something about my works that is technical, or aesthetic or philosophical. Or something: certainly nothing is meant symbolically.

Mendelssohn, on the other hand, is very much of the view that *only* instrumental music is capable of conveying to the listener the meaning which words, for him, obfuscate. Quite what he means by a 'correct' understanding of music, though, is slightly unclear. He knows this: 'Will you allow this to serve as an answer to your question? At all events, it is the only one I can give, – although these too are nothing, after all, but ambiguous words!' A good note on which to turn to the first letter of this chapter.

'SHE IS THE QUEEN OF THE SENSES; WHEN SHE COMES FORTH FROM HER SECRET ABIDING PLACE ALL OTHER THOUGHTS ARE CAST OUT'

CASSIODORUS MUSES UPON THE ANCIENT MYTHOLOGY OF MUSIC

Humans have been enamoured with music for time immemorial. Its relationship with human development has been symbiotic, with archaeological finds of musical instruments dating as far back as the Palaeolithic period. In 2012, for instance, evidence of some of the earliest music ever was discovered in Germany when archaeologists found two flutes, one made from bird bone, the other from mammoth ivory, which were dated to be at least 42,000 years old. Those gifted in the art of music have formed an integral component of even the most ancient of human civilizations, with entire mythologies helping to explain the enchanting influence of music upon the human psyche. In this extraordinary letter written 1,600 years ago, we get a rare glimpse into this age-old human relationship with the otherworldly power of music, as it uncovers the importance of music among the great philosophers and kings of medieval Europe. Moreover, it highlights the enduring influence classical lore and legends had on music and its relationship with humanity.

The letter was written by the Roman statesman and philosopher Magnus Aurelius Cassiodorus Senator (known commonly as Cassiodorus) on behalf of Theodoric the Great, the sixth-century king of the Ostrogoths. He had been charged with fulfilling the request of Clovis, King of the Franks, to have a new *citharoedus* (a lyre player) sent to his court. In order to find the most capable candidate, Cassiodorus (*c.*490–*c.*585) sought the wisdom of the renowned philosopher and theologian Boethius to aid him in his search. Boethius had become a leading authority on musical theory through his work *de institutione musica* ('The Fundamentals of Music'), in which he drew on the philosophies of ancient Greece to theorize the scientific and spiritual workings of music. Cassiodorus was himself a scholar of antiquity, and took the opportunity of writing to Boethius to indulge in some musical theory with one as learned as himself.

The letter gives an enlightening synopsis of the detailed mythology that once surrounded the world of music in ancient Rome and Greece. It tells, for instance, of Orpheus, the legendary bard who journeyed with Jason among his company of Argonauts, and who used his musical powers to soothe the heart of Hades and attempt to save his wife Eurydice from the underworld. Cassiodorus also references the god Mercury (or Hermes in Greece) as the inventor of the lyre, who, it was said, constructed the instrument using a tortoise shell and cow intestines, and later traded the instrument with Apollo, the master musician of the gods.

FRONTISPIECE DEPICTING CASSIODORUS, TWELFTH CENTURY

From Magnus Aurelius Senator Cassiodorus to Anicius Manlius Severinus Boethius, on behalf of King Theodoric, sixth century

The King of the Franks has asked us to send him a harper. We felt that in you lay our best chance of complying with his request, because you, being such a lover of music yourself, will be able to introduce us to the right man.

Reflections on the nature of music. She is the Queen of the senses; when she comes forth from her secret abiding place all other thoughts are cast out. Her curative influence on the soul.

The five tones: the Dorian, influencing to modesty and purity; the Phrygian to fierce combat; the Aeolian to tranquillity and slumber; the Ionian (Jastius), which sharpens the intellect of the dull and kindles the desire of heavenly things; the Lydian, which soothes the soul oppressed with too many cares.

We distinguish the highest, middle and lowest in each tone, obtaining thus in all fifteen tones of artificial music.

The diapason [instrument] is collected from all, and unites all their virtues.

Classical instances of music:

Orpheus.

Amphion.

Musaeus.

The human voice as an instrument of music. Oratory and Poesy as branches of the art.

The power of song: Ulysses and the Sirens.

David the author of the Psalter, who by his melody three times drove away the evil spirit from Saul.

The lyre is called 'chorda', because it so easily moves the hearts (*corda*) of men.

As the diadem dazzles by the variegated lustre of its gems, so the lyre with its divers sounds.

The lyre, the loom of the Muses.

Mercury, the inventor of the lyre, is said to have derived the idea of it from the harmony of the spheres. This astral music, apprehended by reason alone, is said to form one of the delights of heaven. If philosophers had placed that enjoyment not in sweet sounds but in the contemplation of the Creator, they would have spoken fitly; for there is truly joy without end, eternity abiding for ever without weariness, and the mere contemplation of the Divinity produces such happiness that nothing can surpass it. This Being furnishes the true immortality; this heaps delight upon delight; and as outside of Him no creature can exist, so without Him changeless happiness cannot be.

We have indulged ourselves in a pleasant digression, because it is always agreeable to talk of learning with the learned; but be sure to get us that *Citharoedus*, who will go forth like another Orpheus to charm the beast-like hearts of the Barbarians. You will thus both obey us and render yourself famous.

'THE BODY IS TRULY THE GARMENT OF THE SOUL, WHICH HAS A LIVING VOICE; FOR THAT REASON IT IS FITTING THAT THE BODY SIMULTANEOUSLY WITH THE SOUL REPEATEDLY SING PRAISES TO GOD THROUGH THE VOICE'

HILDEGARD OF BINGEN PROTESTS HER DIVINE RIGHT TO SING

In the year 1178, the 80-year-old German abbess Hildegard of Bingen received a powerful vision from God. As a mystic believed to possess the power to personally communicate with the heavens, Hildegard (c. 1098–1179) was by no means unaccustomed to such an experience. So regularly did she receive these visions that she even created her own alphabet for the *lingua ignota*, or 'unknown language', that she used to converse with the divine.

In the case of this particular vision, however, Hildegard found herself presented with a major theological dilemma. A voice compelled her to ignore the conditions of the interdict under which her convent had been placed by the prelates acting on behalf of the Archbishop of Mainz. The decision to impose an interdict had been made after Hildegard had allowed an excommunicated nobleman to be buried in holy ground, and it forbade her from performing worship of any kind, including the singing of sacraments. If Hildegard were to heed the divine message to disregard this injunction, she would run the very real risk of being excommunicated from the Christian church. Faced with this divine intervention, however, Hildegard felt she had no choice but to defend her right to sing God's praises.

The vision presents a fascinating intersection between Hildegard's powers of mysticism and her passion for religious music. Despite professing to have had no formal training, she was a prolific composer, producing over 70 pieces of religious music. Akin to her visions, Hildegard identified divine inspiration as the source for her compositions, a relationship reflected in the title of her collected works: *symphoniae harmoniae celestium revelationum* ('The Harmonious Music of Celestial Revelations'). In music, Hildegard found a tangible expression of God's presence in the world. It is a conduit to the divine, presenting a medium through which humanity can experience here on earth the euphoria of God's heavenly kingdom. Following the interdict, however, Hildegard found herself excluded from these celestial pleasures. By restricting her ability to perform music, Hildegard believed the prelates were preventing her from spiritually connecting with heaven, and so denying in turn the will of God. Thus, in an act of protest, Hildegard wrote to Mainz extolling the holy virtue of music in the hope of appealing to the prelates' better judgement, and freeing her convent from the spiritual void in which they had been placed.

A FRONTISPIECE FROM *SCIVIAS* DEPICTING HILDEGARD RECEIVING
A VISION FROM GOD, C. 1152

From Hildegard of Bingen to the Prelates of Mainz, 1178/79

... In order not to live as disobedients [*sic*] separated from the whole,
we have left off singing the chants of the Divine Offices exactly
according to the interdict, and we have abstained from participation
in the Body of our Lord, whereas we celebrated it together every
single month according to our general custom. So that above all
for this reason, while I as well as all of my sisters was struck down

with such great bitterness, held back by such monstrous harshness, and suppressed at length by such tremendous weight of authority, I heard these words in a vision . . . And I heard the voice which comes from the living light bringing forth the different forms of praise, about which David sang in the psalms: 'Praise Him in the sound of the trumpet; praise Him in the psalterium and cithra' [sic] etc., to which was added: 'Let every spirit praise the Lord' (Psalm 150). In these words we are instructed about the interior life through exterior things: namely, just how to give form to the Offices serving the interior of human beings and direct them as much as possible towards the praises of the Creator, whether according to the setting of the texts or the nature of the instruments...

The holy prophets, mindful of that divine sweetness and praise through which Adam rejoices in God before the Fall, but not in his exile, wanted also to be aroused to these things themselves. So these prophets, taught by the very spirit they had received, composed not only psalms and canticles which were sung in order to kindle the devotion of the listeners, but also they created various instruments for the art of music. In this way they were able to bring forth a whole variety of sounds as much from the structure and properties of each instrument, as well as from the sense of the words . . .

Clearly in imitation of the holy prophets, the studious and wise, through this same art, invented several kinds of instruments so that what they wanted to sing they could sing to the delight of their souls, by joining their hands while bending with the modulations of their voices. In this way can they also recall Adam (formed by the hand of God which is the Holy Spirit), in whose voice was the tone of every melody and the sweetness of the totality of musical arts before he transgressed and would have remained, were he still in the state in which he was created . . .

Moreover, when that deceiver, the Devil, heard that man began to sing through the inspiration of God, and in this way he was summoned to practise again the sweetness of the chants of the heavenly fatherland . . . then even in the heart of the Church and wherever he [the Devil] was able, whether through dissension and scandal or unjust oppression, he continually disrupted the manifestation and beauty of the psalms and hymns . . .

It is necessary that you pay attention to this so that you are drawn to this same devotion to the justice of God without the desire for punishment and revenge that comes from indignation or an unjust feeling of the heart, and it is always necessary to beware that in your judgements you are not possessed by Satan, who took man away from the heavenly music and from the delights of paradise. Therefore consider carefully that just as the body of Christ was born of the Holy Spirit from the integrity of the Virgin Mary, just so is the song of praise according to the heavenly music radiated by the Holy Spirit in the Church. The body is truly the garment of the soul, which has a living voice; for that reason it is fitting that the body simultaneously with the soul repeatedly sing praises to God through the voice.

In accordance with this meaning the prophetic spirit orders that God be praised with cymbals of jubilation and with the rest of the musical instruments which the wise studious have created, since all of the arts (whose purpose is to fill uses and needs of man) are brought to life by that breath of life which God breathed into the body of man: and therefore it is just that God be praised in all things . . . The prophecy in the psalm . . . exhorts us to confess ourselves to God in the cithara as we sing psalms with the ten-string harp; desiring to restore ourselves, let sound the cithara whose purpose on earth is to train the body; let sound the psalterium which gives back the sound from the heavenly realm above for expanding the spirit; let sound the ten-string harp for contemplation of the law. Therefore, those of the Church who have imposed silence on the singing of the chants for the praise of God without well-considered weight of reason so that they have unjustly stripped God of the grace and comeliness of His own praise, unless they will have freed themselves from their errors here on earth, will be without the company of the angelic songs of praise in heaven.

'THERE IS SO MUCH TALK ABOUT MUSIC, AND YET SO LITTLE REALLY SAID. FOR MY PART I BELIEVE THAT WORDS DO NOT SUFFICE FOR SUCH A PURPOSE'

FELIX MENDELSSOHN EXPLAINS THE EXCEPTIONAL POWER OF MUSICAL EXPRESSION

There are some words that simply cannot be translated into other languages. Take for instance the Inuit word *Iktsuarpok*, which describes the annoyance caused by waiting on an expected guest, or *Razbliuto*, the Russian word used to describe the complex feelings held for a past lover. In such words we see illustrated the distinct nature of each language as a form of communication, and our inability to translate them reminds us of the diversity of human expression. It is by these same principles that music functions.

The emotion and meaning incited by music can escape even the most articulate of speakers. Indeed, music is a medium of expression so visceral and peculiar that to try and qualify it verbally can often prove a futile endeavour. It is, in other words, a whole language in and of itself, and one spoken by musicians to express those emotions they feel unable to articulate in any other way. Such, at least, was the opinion expressed by Felix Mendelssohn in the letter he wrote to his friend Marc-André Souchay in 1842 concerning the composition of his piano pieces *Songs Without Words*.

In the letter, Mendelssohn responded to Souchay's suggestion that the composer should consider turning his piano music into *Lieder* — that is, set the music to poetry. In reply, Mendelssohn tries to explain the fruitlessness of such a proposal. It is not a question of reconstituting the meaning of the music linguistically, but of the meaning of the music being inherent within each piece. To try and capture the meaning of each song in words would be to dilute, or misconstrue, the potency of the original expression. Equally, the subjectivity with which that meaning is received by each listener means that to produce a finite definition for the song using lyrics would only further diminish the impact of the piece. Sometimes, Mendelsohn suggests, it is wisest to avoid words altogether, and trust in music's unique qualities as a medium of expression.

From Felix Mendelssohn to Marc-André Souchay, 1842

Berlin, October 15th, 1842.

. . . There is so much talk about music, and yet so little really said. For my part I believe that words do not suffice for such a purpose, and if I found they did suffice, then I certainly would have nothing more to do with music. People often complain that music is ambiguous, that their ideas on the subject always seem so vague, whereas everyone understands words; with me it is exactly the reverse; not merely with regard to entire sentences, but also as to individual words; these, too, seem to me so ambiguous, so vague, so unintelligible when compared with genuine music, which fills the soul with a thousand things better than words. What the music I love expresses to me, is not thought too *indefinite* to be put into words, but, on the contrary, too *definite*. I therefore consider every effort to express such thoughts commendable, but still there is something unsatisfactory too in them all, and so it is with yours also. This, however, is not your fault, but that of the poetry, which does not enable you to do better. If you ask me what my idea is, I say – just the song as it stands; and if I have in my mind a definite term or terms with regard to one or more of these songs, I will disclose them to no-one, because the words of one person assume a totally different meaning in the mind of another person, because the music of the song alone can awaken the same ideas and the same feelings in one mind as in another, – a feeling which is not, however, expressed by the same words. Resignation, melancholy, the praise of God, a hunting-song, – one person does not form the same conception from these that another does. Resignation is to the one, what melancholy is to the other; the third can form no lively idea of either. To any man who is by nature a very keen sportsman, a hunting-song and the praise of God would come pretty much to the same thing, and to such a one the sound of the hunting-horn would really and truly be the praise of God, while we hear nothing in it but a mere hunting-song; and if we were to discuss it ever so often with him, we should get no further. Words have many meanings, and yet music we could both understand correctly. Will you allow this to serve as an answer to your question? At all events, it is the only one I can give, – although these too are nothing, after all, but ambiguous words!

'I AM CONVINCED THAT TEN YEARS HENCE CARMEN WILL BE THE MOST POPULAR OPERA IN THE WORLD'

TCHAIKOVSKY, BIZET AND THE RISE OF *CARMEN*

On the night of 3 June 1875, the composer Georges Bizet passed away, convinced that his final opera had been a failure. The opera was called *Carmen*, and it had been adapted from a novella of the same name written by the French author Prosper Mérimée. It tells the ill-fated tale of Don José, whose broken heart leads him to murder Carmen, a spirited gypsy dancer, after she rejects him for the dashing torero Escamillo. The dramatic tale immediately caught Bizet's imagination, and with the help of librettists Henri Meilhac and Ludovic Halévy he set about composing a score.

By the time the opera was finished in 1874, Bizet (1838–75) was sure it was some of his finest work. On the night of its debut performance on 3 March 1875, however, the opera's proletarian themes failed to resonate with its bourgeois Parisian audience. Halévy, for instance, who had held reservations about the opera since rehearsals, observed how the audience became more and more muted with each act. By the fourth act they had become 'frigid', and both he had Bizet walked home from the opera with heavy hearts.

For Bizet, the floundering debut of this most cherished of works only added to a list of near misses, and the disappointment triggered a deep bout of depression. Though romantic, the folkloric notion that the opera's failure led to Bizet's early demise at 36 – three months to the day after the opera's opening night – has now begun to be questioned. Nonetheless, there is the overriding sense that he died before his musical potential could be fully realized.

For all the negative press that surrounded *Carmen* in France, however, there were some who saw the opera rather differently. In fact, on one Russian composer by the name of Pyotr Ilyich Tchaikovsky the opera would have a profound effect. From the moment he read the opera, Tchaikovsky was completely enamoured with Bizet and his work, and on finally seeing the opera live on 20 January 1876 he was utterly spellbound.

Even after nearly five years the strength of his admiration had not dulled. Writing here to his friend and patron Nadezhda von Meck, Tchaikovsky explained how he could not help but be overwhelmed with emotion when replaying the opera.

Sure enough, Tchaikovsky's prediction of *Carmen's* fame would prove prophetic. Today, the opera is heralded as one of the finest ever written, and is one of the most regularly performed worldwide.

From Pyotr Ilyich Tchaikovsky to Madame Nadezhda von Meck, 1880

Simaki, July 18th (30th), 1880.

Yesterday evening – to take a rest from my own work – I played through Bizet's *Carmen* from cover to cover. I consider it a *chef-d'oeuvre* in the fullest sense of the word: one of those rare compositions which seem to reflect most strongly the musical tendencies of a whole generation. It seems to me that our own period differs from earlier ones in this one characteristic: that contemporary composers *are engaged in the pursuit of charming and piquant effects*, unlike Mozart, Beethoven, Schubert or Schumann.

What is the so-called New Russian School but the cult of varied and pungent harmonies, of original orchestral combinations and every kind of purely external effect? Musical ideas give place to this or that union of sounds. Formerly there was *composition, creation*; now (with few exceptions) there is only research and invention. This development of musical thought is naturally purely intellectual, consequently contemporary music is clever, piquant and eccentric; but cold and lacking the glow of true emotion. And behold, a Frenchman comes on the scene, in whom these qualities of piquancy and pungency are not the outcome of effort and reflection, but flow from his pen as in a free stream, flattering the ear, but touching us also. It is as though he said to us: 'You ask nothing great, superb, or grandiose – you want something *pretty*, here is a *pretty opera*'; and truly I know of nothing in music which is more representative of that element which I call *the pretty* (*le joli*) . . . I cannot play the last scene without tears in my eyes; the gross rejoicings of the crowd who look on at the bull-fight, and, side by side with this, the poignant tragedy and death of the two principal characters, pursued by an evil fate, who come to their inevitable end through a long series of sufferings.

I am convinced that ten years hence *Carmen* will be the most popular opera in the world. But no-one is a prophet in his own land. In Paris *Carmen* has had no real success.

'I DO NOT WANT TO BE UNDERSTOOD – I WANT TO EXPRESS MYSELF – BUT I HOPE I WILL BE MISUNDERSTOOD. IT WOULD BE TERRIBLE IF PEOPLE COULD SEE THROUGH ME'

ARNOLD SCHOENBERG ON THE MEANING OF MUSIC BETWEEN COMPOSER AND AUDIENCE

For a musician who was almost entirely self-taught, the composer Arnold Schoenberg made a remarkable impact on musical theory in the twentieth century. He was ever the innovator, bringing the first tenets of the expressionist movement to music through his atonal style and pioneering the 12-tone technique. Schoenberg (1874–1951) also wrote extensively on the topic of composition, publishing several influential texts, including *Harmonielehre (Theory of Harmony*, 1922).

His approach to composition made him a controversial figure, however, with some dismissing him as a radical while others deemed him revolutionary (especially his students Alban Berg and Anton Webern). For a man so outspoken on the nature of composition, however, it appears Schoenberg was anxious not to allow himself to be revealed by the music he produced.

Evidence of Schoenberg's secretive relationship with his music can be seen in the letter he wrote to his fellow composer Alma Mahler in the Autumn of 1910. Schoenberg had sought Alma's critical feedback on a composition he was currently working on (possibly the melodrama *Pierrot Lunaire*), and her advice caused Schoenberg to reflect on how meaning manifests within his music.

In line with the philosophy of expressionism within art, Schoenberg promotes a subjective conception of music which sits in tandem with his desire for audiences to think critically about the music he produced. If his music does not manifest in the minds of performers or audiences in the way he had intended, then all the better. Music is there to be mused on, and the plurality of emotion it can trigger sits at the heart of its beauty.

ARNOLD SCHOENBERG

From Arnold Schoenberg to Alma Mahler, 1910

7 October 1910

Very esteemed Madam,

Thank you very much for your letter. It pleases me a great deal that my piece already meant something to you in this unfinished form, because I hope that, when you will see it in its entirety, it will be able to say to you what I really wanted to express. What one calls 'thinking' is *not at all* what I was thinking about; but I certainly surmised that many things can be imagined from it. If I should be honest and say something about my works (which I prefer not to do because I really write them to conceal myself, so as not to be seen), thus it could only be this: it is not meant symbolically, but rather only viewed and felt. Not at all thought. Colours, noises, lights, sounds, movements, glances, gestures – in short, the media that constitute the material of the stage – should be juxtaposed in a variegated manner. Nothing else. – As I wrote it down, according to my feeling, it signified something to me. If the components, when assembled, produce a similar image, that would be agreeable to me. If not, so much the better. Because I do not want to be understood – I want to express myself – but I hope I will be misunderstood. It would be terrible if people could see through me. For this reason I prefer to say something about my works that is technical, or aesthetic, or philosophical. Or something: certainly nothing is meant symbolically. It is all unmediated perception. Perhaps you will best be able to understand my intentions when I tell you that I could most like to write for a magic theatre. If tones, when they are ranged in some way, are able to evoke feelings, then colours, gestures, movements must also be capable of that. Even if they do not make any kind of perceivable sense. Music does not make either! - Thus I mean: that is music!

Again, heartfelt thanks!

And now: tomorrow (Saturday) my exhibition with Heller opens. Can you go? Wednesday evening is the concert. I would be very happy if you could be there.

I would also like to know how it (the drama) pleases the Director. Probably not! But hopefully a little. If only it does not appear ridiculous to him. At the moment I have no confidence in myself.

I am very much looking forward to Sunday. And if nothing adverse and sickening prevents me, I will be there.

With many devoted heartfelt greetings,

Arnold Schoenberg

NB: I am sending you my new piano pieces.

'I AM REALIZING THAT MERE SOCIAL WORK WON'T REPLACE THE MUSIC – ONLY PACIFIST WITNESS AGAINST THE WHOLE MADNESS CAN DO SO'

MICHAEL TIPPETT STAYS TRUE TO HIS CONVICTIONS

On 3 February 1942, the composer Michael Tippett (1905–98) was summoned before the members of the South East London Tribunal to hear their judgement on his application to be formally registered as a conscientious objector. The tribunal had three options: they could grant him unconditional registration, absolving him of any legal responsibility to support the war effort; conditional registration, requiring non-combative duties such as work with the Air Raid Precautions or the Fire Service; or dismiss his application and order him to join the military. To refuse the last two of these judgements held the risk of a jail sentence.

To Tippett's dismay, the members of the tribunal opted for the second of these three judgements: non-combative military service. The judgement presented Tippett with a terrible moral dilemma: he could compromise, accept their judgement and support the war effort, but to do so, however, would be to betray his convictions as a pacifist. Tippett was a lifelong advocate for the tenets of humanism, and had quickly joined the Peace Pledge Union (a pacifist campaigning organization of which he would later become President) following his call-up for military service in 1940. Conversely, to refuse the tribunal's decision brought the risk being sent to prison, a fate that jeopardized his future as a musician.

Still reeling from the tribunal's verdict, Tippett wrote to his friend, the writer, musician and fellow pacifist Francesca Allinson, to report the troubled days of soul searching he had endured.

Ultimately, Tippett reached the agonizing conclusion that nothing short of outright refusal would suffice for sacrificing his identity as a musician. With the world at war, he believed, it was now more important than ever to stay true to his pacifist convictions. So, with the reassuring knowledge that his friends would do all they could to sustain his musical career in the event of his imprisonment, Tippett decided to appeal the tribunal's decision. In response, the tribunal offered instead the choice to work for the air or fire services. Still Tippett refused, and so on 21 June 1943 he was sentenced to three months' imprisonment.

In the end, Tippett only served one month of his sentence on account of good behaviour. Moreover, his time in prison proved to be an incredibly enriching experience, one which not only assured him of his pacifism, but also made him resolute in his work as a composer. His famous oratorio *Child of Our Time*, for instance, composed between 1939 and 1941, is a piece that celebrates the synthesis of his identity as both musician and a pacifist.

SIR MICHAEL TIPPETT (LEFT) ATTENDING A REHEARSAL FOR HIS
BIRTHDAY CONCERT WITH CONDUCTOR COLIN DAVIS, 1975

From Michael Tippett to Francesca Allinson, 1942

6 February 1942

Fresca darling —

Hope you do come up Monday — I want to see you badly and I am up
Tuesday, Wed., Thurs., sleeping in town Tuesd. — Wed. — the first with
Mrs [Eva] Hubback, the second at David [Ayerst]'s — or *anderswo*. The
Hubback date is due to Tribunal matters — I went last Tuesday and to
everyone's surprise lost! Non-combatant military duties. There was
the initial shock that a person of my quality can't get by while the
Wilfs [Franks — his lover] etc can — but subsequently when I got home
and began to realise in my body that the music must go whichever
way I travel, I cried like a child. Now I feel better, but lost. David and
everyone almost else, is trying to get me to compromise — but I am
realising that mere social work won't replace the music — only pacifist
witness against the whole madness can do so. I am going through
a considerable moral crisis and on the issue will depend whether I
can witness outside or inside quod. I am not frightened by quod any
more — but my friends are for me. I intend to do that thing which will
most clearly show the measure of the world debacle, now that my
own island has been shattered. It will only be for a time, whatever I
decide to do. Mercifully, as Evelyn says, a portion of my musical self
has got out into the big world and Goehr and others willing to hold
its baby hand while poppa is away from home. I want very much to
have the know that things will go on for that side of me by my friends
while I am doing my other, enforced job of witness — that will make
everything ever so much easier. Goehr has already assured me — and
he is very grateful for all I have done for him — he intends to play my
music wherever he can, especially if I am not there. So I shan't feel so
desperately lost and lonely. Look — ring me when you can and we'll
meet Tuesday or Wed. or Thurs.

love

M.

'WHETHER I EVER UNFOLD THE WINGS AND MAKE A START TOWARD THE STRATOSPHERE AND HOW MUCH OF THE DUST OF THE ROAD WILL STILL CLING TO ME, IS AN INTERESTING QUESTION, AT LEAST TO ME'

RUTH CRAWFORD SEEGER REFLECTS ON HER IDENTITY AS COMPOSER

When Ruth Crawford Seeger (1901–53) landed in Paris in 1930, she arrived as one of America's most promising composers. For the past nine years she had been studying music and composition at the American Conservatory of Music in Chicago, and it was during this time that she began to attract attention for her experimental style.

From the very beginning of her career, Crawford was deeply inspired by the teachings of such modernist composers as Arnold Schoenberg, and these influences expressed themselves in the formalism and serialism prevalent in many of her early compositions (such as Music for Small Orchestra, 1926). Dissonant counterpoint was also an area of intrigue for the young composer, an interest nurtured by her teacher and future husband, Charles Seeger. By this principle, a composer avoids the traditional intervals found in Western music, such as thirds, sixths or fifths, to produce music that challenges the conventions of compositional theory. Working with these core concepts, Crawford in turn developed her own innovations to build a unique style which extended serialism to aspects of music such as dynamics and form, and this distinctive sound helped her become the first woman to receive the prestigious Guggenheim Fellowship, so laying the way for her passage to Paris. Crawford continued to refine her compositional style in Europe, and it was during this time that she composed her most critically acclaimed piece, the String Quartet, in 1931.

Only one year later, however, in 1932, Ruth's career as a composer came to an abrupt halt when she married Charles Seeger. As well as a teacher, Seeger was a musicologist with a passion for preserving the musical heritage of America, and following their marriage Crawford joined him on the road in search of the soul of American music. Such research undoubtedly made an invaluable contribution to the preservation of America's folk traditions. For Crawford, however, taking part in this endeavour came at the heavy price of capping her potential as a composer.

The letter seen here was sent in response to one sent to Crawford by modernist composer Edgard Varèse. In it, he asked Crawford to choose which of her compositions she felt was 'most representative' of her style, as well as a note on her musical 'credo'. In return, Crawford highlights the duality to her character which made it so difficult to answer these questions. Using the wonderful metaphor of flight, she captures the conflicting spheres of her passions and ambitions. She grapples not only with the prospect of whether she will ever return to composing, but also the question of if she were to, the extent to which she will have been changed by her experience of being on the road exploring American folk music. Despite her doubts, Crawford nonetheless managed to detail the core components of her philosophy towards composition.

From Ruth Crawford Seeger to Edgard Varèse, 1948

May 29, 1948

Dear Edgard Varèse:

Your first letter saying you wanted to include me in your course at Columbia was dated January 8. I ought to wait ten more days to make it exactly five months. I hope my lateness has not inconvenienced you too greatly. It seems that everything has combined to make this spring full. Teaching at two schools, plus a full private-teaching schedule (including an 8 till 6 Saturday), plus work on a book which is coming out this fall, plus proof on the Lomax* book which

---

*Alan Lomax was the doyen of field researchers on American folk music.

came out this spring, plus four healthy children-and-a-house, have combined to emphasize my natural indolence as to letter writing.

One reason I have been late in answering is, that you asked for a kind of 'credo'. I found that a little hard, for I am still not sure whether the road I have been following the last dozen years is a main road or a detour. I have begun to feel, the past year or two, that it is the latter – a detour, but a very important one to me, during which I have descended from stratosphere onto a solid well-traveled [*sic*] highway, folded my wings and breathed good friendly dust as I travelled along in and out of the thousands of fine traditional folktunes [*sic*] which I have been hearing and singing and transcribing from field-recordings, for books and for pleasure. Until a year or so ago I had felt so at home among this (to me) new found music that I thought maybe this was what I wanted most. I listened to nothing else, and felt somewhat like a ghost when my compositions were spoken of. I answered no letters pertaining to them; requests for scores and biographical data were stuck in drawers. There were, of course, occasional periods during which I returned to composition, as for instance when CBS wanted works for orchestra utilizing folk material for performance on the 'School of the Air'. Charlie and I were among those commissioned, and his *John Henry* and my *Rissolty Rossolty* were performed there in 1941. But for years the only instrument in the house was a guitar, a modern dulcimer and a special slow-speed phonograph for transcription of folk recordings.

Whether I ever unfold the wings and make a start toward the stratosphere and how much of the dust of the road will still cling to me, is an interesting question, at least to me. If I do, I will probably pull the road up with me.

As for a 'credo' typifying my music of the type of [the] String Quartet (1931) and Three Songs for Contralto and Orchestra, which ISCM chose for [the] Amsterdam festival back in 1933, I could mention a few points about which I felt strongly. And I still feel strongly about them. I believe when I write more music these elements will be there, or at least striven for:

Clarity of melodic line
Avoidance of rhythmic stickiness
Rhythmic independence between parts
Feeling of tonal and rhythmic center
Experiment with various means of obtaining, at the same time, organic unity and various sorts of dissonance.

As to works which I consider most representative, I am inclined to choose the String Quartet (1931). It is the slow movement of this quartet which was recorded on New Music Recordings, a copy of which Mrs Varèse says you have. I am sending the score of this quartet, with the third and fourth movements analysed as to tone, rhythm, form and dynamics. I would like to mention that the recording was made at rather short notice, and that therefore the counterpoint of the crescendos, mentioned in the analysis, is not well heard on the recording.

A few of the things Charlie and I have been doing since 1935 may be of interest as a backdrop. We have four children, said by our friends to have both charm and good looks, born in 1933, '35, '37, and '44: Michael, Peggy, Barbara and Penelope. When Barbara went to co-operative nursery school in 1941 I went with her, and a book, *American Folk Songs for Children*, grew out of the experience (to come out this fall, Doubleday). Previous to this I worked as music editor on the Lomax *Our Singing Country*, which involved transcription to musical notation of several hundred traditional songs, and the listening to many hundred more in [the] process of choosing these for publication. In connection with this I worked on a sixty-page treatise on the music of these songs, [which was] never quite finished nor published. This work really grew out of Charlie's activities as technical advisor in the Special Skills Division of the Resettlement Administration, and our close acquaintance with the music we heard everywhere during our travels among and to and from the resettlement colonies.

We have acted as consultants for several publishing houses, in American folk music for children I also planned and chose the music for the State Department for a series of radio broadcasts, "Music in American Life." Last summer Charlie and I, with Dr Emrich of the Archive of American Folklore, Library of Congress, completed a book of 900 American traditional songs, to be published by Dial Press, half of them we transcribed from field recordings. And this spring another Lomax book, *Folksong: USA*, was published by Duell Sloan Pearce, with 111 accompaniments by us.

Charlie joins me in warm good wishes from us both. Perhaps next time I come to New York I can know far enough in advance to be less spontaneous in getting in touch with you.

Cordially,

Ruth Crawford Seeger

'ANY MUSIC WHICH COULD GROW AND PROPAGATE ITSELF AS OUR MUSIC HAS, MUST HAVE A HELL OF AN AFFIRMATIVE BELIEF INHERENT IN IT'

JOHN COLTRANE EXPLAINS WHAT IT MEANS TO BE A JAZZ MUSICIAN

In the small hours of the morning when many of the patrons of Philadelphia's nightclub scene had grown whisky-weary and retreated from the dance floor, one man and his saxophone were able to cut through the cigarette haze, enlivening the crowds with his experimental riffs of brooding, sultry jazz.

John Coltrane's fiercely unique style led him to become known as one of the most legendary jazz musicians of the twentieth century, and his improvisational innovations set the blueprint for jazz saxophonists for generations to come.

Coltrane (1926–67) was a musician who had to be seen live for the brilliance of his music to be fully appreciated. So compelling was his sound, and so visceral the energy his music conjured for its listeners, that since his death in 1967 Coltrane has been venerated as a saint by the African Orthodox Church in San Francisco; for them it is evident God 'dwells in the musical majesty of his sounds'.

Starting out as a horn for hire, Coltrane grasped every opportunity to hone his skill as a saxophonist, and the instrument served as a crutch for the many hardships he experienced early in his life. In his formative years he had the incredible opportunity to cut his teeth playing in the bands of the greatest names in jazz, including Dizzy Gillespie, Duke Ellington and Miles Davis. Unsurprisingly, these experiences proved instrumental in Coltrane's development as a musician. His time with Miles Davis in particular – whose band he joined in 1955 – left a lasting impression, spurring on his creativity.

In 1960 Coltrane finally emerged from among the shadows of the big jazz bands with his recording of 'My Favorite Things'. It was a pivotal moment in his career, reflecting not only the maturity of his personal sound and style, but also his skill as a band leader. The track proved highly popular, and its success crowned a period of personal growth for the musician that had commenced in 1957. According to Coltrane, it was in this year that he experienced a Christian spiritual awakening. It enabled him to kick for good the heroin addiction that had so far dogged his career, and set him on a righteous path of musical discovery. From this point onwards, Coltrane was dedicated to a life of musical and spiritual enlightenment.

Two years on from this watershed moment, Coltrane came to reflect on what it meant to be a jazz musician in a letter to journalist, Don DeMicheal. Musing on the writings of Aaron Copland, Coltrane challenged the idea that the social relevance of music had waned; rather the experience of the musician was entirely dependent on the music they played. In the case of the jazz musician, there is no doubt as to the relevance of their music. It is a sound with an inextinguishable vitality fed constantly by the musicians who play it, which never fails to resonate with audiences worldwide.

JOHN COLTRANE IN PERFORMANCE, 1960S

From John Coltrane to Don DeMicheal, 1962

June 2, 1962

Dear Don,

Many thanks for sending Aaron Copland's fine book, *Music and Imagination*. I found it historically revealing and on the whole, quite informative. However, I do not feel that all of his tenets are *entirely* essential or applicable to the 'jazz' musician. This book seems to be written more for the American classical or semi-classical composer who has the problem, as Copland sees it, of not finding himself an integral part of the musical community, or having difficulty in finding a positive philosophy or justification for his art. The 'jazz' musician (you can have this term along with several others that have been foisted upon us) does not have this problem at all. We have absolutely no reason to worry about lack of positive and affirmative philosophy. It's built in us. The phrasing, the sound of the music attest this fact. We are naturally endowed with it. You can believe all of us would have perished long ago if this were not so. As to community, the whole face of the globe is our community. You see, it is really easy for us to create. We are born with this feeling that just comes out no matter what conditions exist. Otherwise, how could our founding fathers have produced this music in the first place when they surely found themselves (as many of us do today) existing in hostile communities where there was everything to fear and damn few to trust. Any music which could grow and propagate itself as our music has, must have a hell of an affirmative belief inherent in it. Any person who claims to doubt this, claims to believe that the exponents of our music of freedom are not guided by this same entity, is either prejudiced, musically sterile, just plain stupid or scheming. Believe me, Don, we all know that this word which so many seem to fear today, 'Freedom' has a hell of a lot to do with this music. Anyway, I did find in Copland's book many fine points. For example: 'I cannot imagine an art work without implied convictions.' – Neither can I. I am sure that you and many others have enjoyed and garnered much of value from this well written book.

If I may, I would like to express a sincere hope that in the near future, a vigorous investigation of the materials presented in this book and others related will help cause an opening up of the ears that are still closed to the progressive music created by the independent thinking artist of today. When this is accomplished, I am certain that the owners of such ears will easily recognize the very vital and highly enjoyable qualities that exist in this music. I also feel that through such honest endeavor, the contributions of future creators will be more easily recognized, appreciated and enjoyed; particularly by the listener who may otherwise miss the point (intellectually, emotionally, sociologically, etc.) because of inhibitions, a lack of understanding, limited means of association or other reasons.

You know, Don, I was reading a book on the life of Van Gogh today, and I had to pause and think of that wonderful and persistent force – the creative urge. The creative urge was in this man who found himself so much at odds with the world he lived in, and in spite of all the adversity, frustrations, rejections and so forth – beautiful and living art came forth abundantly . . . if only he could be here today. Truth is indestructible. It seems history shows (and it's the same way today) that the innovator is more often than not met with some degree of condemnation; usually according to the degree of his departure from the prevailing modes of expression or what have you. Change is always so hard to accept. We also see that these innovators always seek to revitalize, extend and reconstruct the status quo in their given fields, wherever it is needed. Quite often they are the rejects, outcasts, sub-citizens, etc. of the very societies to which they bring so much sustenance. Often they are people who endure great personal tragedy in their lives. Whatever the case, whether accepted or rejected, rich or poor, that are forever guided by that great and eternal constant – the creative urge. Let us cherish it and give all praise to God. Thank you and best wishes to all.

Sincerely,

P.S. Congratulations to the writer of Article, 'Thunder in the Wings'. I think it was Bill Mathieu. He is consistently proving himself one of the best in music theory. Thanks also to Martin Williams for his very fine discourse in the same issue.

CHAPTER FOUR

COMPOSITION

It is most certainly true that of those composers we idolize today, each and every one of them is in possession of something exceeding skill. What that 'something' is, however, remains unclear, even to some composers themselves, as we discover in Edvard Grieg's wilfully terse response to a letter enquiring as to his creative process: 'I should think it quite impossible to answer your questions 1) as I have no method at all when composing!'

Despite the reluctance of some composers to discuss their methods, it is something every musician must at least attempt to grasp on whatever visceral level that may be if they are to succeed – just as performance and the inner qualities of music must in some way be understood.

Composition is the act of creating – out of nothing – a musical work. This can be an act in itself, carried out by the composer in the privacy of their home with a blank sheet of manuscript paper and perhaps a piano; or it can be almost indistinguishable from performance if a work is, as it were, conjured from thin air at the moment of performance – think of some jazz, or of the great French tradition of organ improvisation. In the case of Western art music at least, this act of creation is defined by the composer utilizing their skills to create an artwork, and so create a visual depiction of that artwork in the form of a score that can be used for future performances. It is, as such, *their* work, played *their* way, for many centuries to come.

To become a composer within this musical tradition is a decision usually made fairly early on in a musician's career. Whether it be at a university or a conservatoire, these individuals will, as pupils, train to acquire all the necessary tools to make them capable composers. Some could emerge with a portfolio within which is found the beginnings of a new, fresh 'voice' in art-music composition.

It is not only by formal instruction that the art of composition can be acquired, however. Rather it is also something that can be learned beyond the realms of the academy ad hoc, and practised, so to say, 'off the cuff'. Nick Cave is one such individual to have taken this unconventional route and, unlike Grieg, is more than willing to delve into what lies beneath the acquired set of skills and abilities of the composer. Cave writes a letter of some beauty which articulates without defining the intangible, almost numinous quality of the moment of artistic, musical creation: a 'shimmering'. But there is a telling passage towards the end of this letter which deftly draws out a thread we find running throughout the chapter. Of that moment when isolated musical ideas begin to be drawn together into something coherent, something with *meaning*, he writes that

> your heart begins to beat as if for the first time in God knows how long, and you come alive, you become an actual person, a functional, competent human being deserving of their place on this earth, because you know, suddenly, more than anything, that you are onto something and this shimmering convergence of words is setting off on its journey to change the world.

The idea of deserving one's place on this earth because of one's compositional output is a revealing sentiment, and one which, among other things, confirms our suspicion that the act of composition is about so much more than simply the use of acquired skills. But in broader terms this is a sentiment about the personal cost of creation. We find it echoed again and again in the letters that make up this chapter, expressed in language sophisticated and simple.

To compose, then, much like to perform, is an act of self-giving; an act which often, as we read from Grieg, from Nick Cave, from Michael Tippett, from Woody Guthrie and others, is difficult fully to comprehend and both emotionally and physically demanding. What results is a creation profoundly connected with the creator's personhood, and criticism or external tampering is dangerous. (Self-criticism is a different, common indulgence: Fanny Mendelssohn and Joseph Haydn turn their fire on themselves without compunction.)

To read the letters in this chapter is to read not of a discrete act, separated from those 'other' elements of what it is to 'do music'. Instead it is to focus as far as is possible on one of those intertwined strands and to accept that, as in a plait, each strand is periodically obscured from view by one of the others. The act of skilled self-giving in which each 'composer' in this chapter invests so much of themselves is a mysterious one. Perhaps we should be content to revel in the mystery.

'I VERY WELL APPROVE OF MR BRIDGE WHO WITHOUT ANY OBJECTION IS A VERY GOOD ORGAN BUILDER . . .'

GEORGE HANDEL'S ORGAN MAKER

The organ is a truly spectacular piece of musical engineering. Consisting of as many as 20,000 pipes or more, between two and five sets of keys for the hands (known as manuals) and a pedal keyboard for the feet, its size alone is enough to warrant Mozart's claim that the organ is the 'king of instruments'.

Notwithstanding its mechanical complexity, however, the true, intricate beauty of the instrument lies in the agency an organ player is afforded in personalizing the sound it produces. The key to this level of customization is the use of what are known as 'stops' – a mechanism which controls the flow of pressurized air into one or more pipes. These stops are numerous and can each be turned on or off, meaning the musician has full control over which sets of pipes are receiving air, or 'wind', at any given time. Such is the level of freedom afforded that, over time, organs began to develop their own national characteristics depending on the combination of stops – or style of 'registration' – favoured in that country.

Today, popular perceptions of the organ associate it either with church music or images of vampires in haunted castles playing Bach's Toccata and Fugue in D minor. In truth, however, the organ is an incredibly versatile instrument, and has been favoured by many of the greatest composers. In England, foremost of these was George Frideric Handel (1685–1759).

Handel's mastery of the organ is indicative of the depths to which he understood the instrument, and he soon came to be regarded as a leading authority on the organ in England. In 1749, one wealthy landowner by the name of Charles Jennens went in search of this expertise when he wrote to Handel requesting his advice on an organ he was having made for his newly renovated stately home. It was a request Handel was more than happy to oblige. Jennens was a close friend and patron who had helped author the librettos for several of his oratorios, including *Messiah*, and Handel was glad to answer his friend's request for consultation.

The letter is littered with terminology entirely alien to anyone unfamiliar with the organ. A 'compass' (also known as a console) is the key desk which holds all the keyboards, pedals and stops; the section from 'open diapason' through to 'flute stop' describes the type of stops Handel recommends be included in the organ registration. Amazingly, the organ survives almost entirely unaltered to this day in the church of St James in Great Packington, Warwickshire.

GEORGE HANDEL PAINTED BY BALTHASAR DENNER, *c.* 1726–8

From George Handel to Charles Jennens, 1749

Sir

Yesterday I received your Letter, in answer to which I hereunder specify my Opinion of an Organ which I think will answer the Ends you propose, being every thing that is necessary for a good and grand organ with Reed Stops, which I have omitted, because they are continually wanting to be tuned, which in the Country is very inconvenient, and should it remain useless on that account it would still be very expensive, altho [*sic*] that may not be your Consideration. I very well approve of Mr Bridge who without any

Objection is a very good Organ Builder, and I shall willingly (when he has finished it) give you my Opinion of it. I have referr'd [*sic*] you to the Flute Stop in Mr Freemans Organ being excellent in its kind, but as I do not refer you in that Organ, The System of the Organ I advise is __

> The Compass to be up to D and down to gamut, full Octave, Church Work,
> One Row of Keys, whole stops and none in halves.
> Stops
> An Open Diapason – of Metal throughout to be in in Front.
> A Stop Diapason – the Treble Metal and the Bass Wood.
> A Principal – of Metal throughout.
> A Twelfth – of metal throughout.
> A fifteenth – of Metal throughout.
> A great Tierce – of Metal throughout.
> A Flute Stop – such a one as in Freemans Organ.

I am glad of the Opportunity to show you my attention, wishing you all Health and Happiness, I remain with great Sincerity and Respect

Sir

your
Most obedient and most humble servant

George Frideric Handel

London. Sept. 30. 1749

Sir

Yesterday I received Your Letter
in answer to which I hereunder specify
my Opinion of an Organ which I think
will answer the Ends you propose, being
every thing that is necessary for a good and
grand Organ without Reed tops, which I have
omitted, because they are continually wanting
to be tuned which in the Country is very
inconvenient, and should it remain useless

on that account, it wou'd still be very expensive
altho' that mey not be your Consideration,
I very well approve of Mr Bridge who
without any Objection is a very good
Organ Builder, and I shall willingly (when
He has finish'd it) give You my Opinion of it.
I have referr'd you to the Flute stop in
Mr Freemans Organ being excellent in
its kind, but as I do not referr you
in that Organ, The System of the
Organ I advise is, (Viz.)

The Compass to be up to D and down to Gamut,
          full Octave,   Church Work,
one Row of Keys, whole stops and none in halves.

Stops

An Open Diapason — of Metal throughout to be in Front.

a Stopt Diapason — the Treble Metal and the Bass Wood.

a Principal — of Metal throughout.

a Twelfth — of Metal throughout.

a Fifteenth — of Metal throughout.

a great Tierce — of Metal throughout.

a Flute Stop — such a one as in Freemans Organ.

I am glad of the Opportunity to show you my attention, wishing you all Health and Happiness, I remain with great Sincerity and Respect

Sir

Your

London. Sept. 30.
1749.

most obedient and most humble
Servant
George Frideric Handel

LETTER FROM GEORGE FRIDERIC HANDEL TO
CHARLES JENNENS, 30 SEPTEMBER 1749. HTTPS://WWW.LOC.GOV/
ITEM/MUSMOLDEN.2774/

'MY MUSIC ONLY TENDS TO ENHANCE THE EXPRESSION, AND TO ADD FORCE TO THE DECLAMATION OF THE POETRY'

THE PHILOSOPHIES OF GLUCK: POETRY AND COMPOSITION

Christoph Willibald Gluck (1714–87) was a composer whose reformist approach to opera made him a leading light of the emerging classicism movement of the eighteenth century. By his innovations, he helped forward a revolution in musical theory that inspired many future greats, the likes of which include Mozart, Hector Berlioz and Wagner. A central tenet of his philosophy was that music and poetry be brought into perfect harmony. Only then could the most compelling expression of drama be performed. Music, in this sense, is an accompaniment, or rather an enhancer, of poetic expression, intended to complement rather than obscure. This, in the context of opera, was the true and original purpose of music.

Gluck's musical talents took him across the length and breadth of Europe. Born in Upper Palatinate (now part of Germany), Gluck began his training in Italy under the tutelage of Giovanni Battista Sammartini before travelling between cities such as London, Prague, Hamburg, Copenhagen and Vienna. In 1773 he arrived in Paris, and it was while in France that Gluck produced many of his most influential operas.

While many welcomed the arrival of this new exciting voice on the Parisian scene, there were others who were more sceptical of the changes he wished to impose on the status quo of Italian opera. Therefore, some groundwork was needed to warm the French public to Gluck's operatic designs. Gluck sent this letter to the editor of the French paper *Mercure de France* in response to one they had printed earlier that year addressed to a director at the Royal Academy of Music in Paris. It had been written by the French diplomat and playwright François-Louis Gand Le Bland Du Roullet, and its purpose was to encourage the opera house to host the debut of Gluck's opera,

Iphigénie in Aulis. The opera was the first of Gluck's to be written in French specifically for the French stage, and its premiere presented an important step for his career in the country. Coincidentally, it just so happened that Du Roullet was the author of the libretto for the opera, and it is likely this public exchange of letters was all part of a well-orchestrated PR stunt to garner public interest in it.

While accepting the praise of Du Roullet, Gluck makes sure to humbly acknowledge the debt he owed to his close collaborator, the Italian poet Ranieri de' Calzabigi. The two had been brought together by their shared desire to reform opera, and this shared goal led to a fruitful creative relationship, with Calzabigi writing the librettos for several of Gluck's operas.

CHRISTOPH WILLIBALD GLUCK BY
JOSEPH-SIFFRED DUPLESSIS, 1775

From Christoph Willibald Gluck to the Editor of the Mecure de France, *1772*

Sir,

I might justly be reproached by others, and should also severely reproach myself, after reading the letter written to one of the directors of the Royal Academy of Music, inserted in your 'Mercury' of last October, the subject of which is 'Iphigenia'— and, after expressing my gratitude to the author of that letter for the praise which he has been pleased to lavish on me – were I not eager to declare that his friendship, and far too favourable impressions of me, have no doubt carried him away, and I am very far from flattering myself that I merit the eulogies he bestows on me. I should reproach myself even more keenly, were I to allow the invention of this new style of Italian opera, the success of which has justified the attempt, to be attributed to myself. The principal merit is due to M. Calzabigi; and if my music has produced any sensation, I ought to acknowledge that it is he who has enabled me to develop the resources of my art. This author, full of genius and talent, has followed a path little known by Italians in his *libretti* of 'Orpheus', 'Alceste' and 'Paride'. These works are overflowing with those happy situations, and terrible and pathetic events, which supply the composer with the means of expressing ardent passion, and creating energetic and touching music. Whatever talent a composer may possess, he can only write indifferent music, if the poet does not excite in him that enthusiasm, without which the productions of every art music be feeble and languid. The imitation of nature is the acknowledged aim which all ought to seek. This it is that I strive to attain; always simple and natural, so far as I can possibly make it so, my music only tends to enhance the expression, and to add force to the declamation of the poetry. For this reason I do not employ those *shakes*, *passages* and *cadences*, of which Italians are so lavish. Their language, therefore, which quite suits this style, is, in this respect, by no means advantageous for me: no doubt it has many other merits, but, born in Germany, I do not consider that any study on my part, of either Italian or French, entitles me to appreciate the delicate shades which cause a preference for one beyond the other, and I think that a foreigner ought to abstain from judging between them; but I may be allowed to say, that the language which suits me best, is that which enables the poet to furnish me with the most varied means of expressing the passions . . .

I request, Sir, that you will be so obliging as to insert this letter into your next 'Mercury'.

I have the honour to be, Sir, &c.,

Chevalier Gluck

'EVERY DAY THE WORLD PAYS ME COMPLIMENTS ON THE FIRE OF MY RECENT WORKS, BUT NO ONE WILL BELIEVE THE STRAIN AND EFFORT IT COSTS ME TO PRODUCE THEM'

HAYDN ON AGEING AND THE GROWING ORDEAL OF COMPOSITION

It certainly cannot be claimed that Joseph Haydn (1732–1809) was an idle man. The Austrian conductor and composer wrote an impressive 107 symphonies, 83 string quartets, 45 piano trios, 62 piano sonatas, 14 masses and 26 operas over the course of his career. He was not only a prolific producer of music, however, but also truly had a brilliant talent for it, and spent much of his life at the beating heart of European classical music.

Haydn's music was defined by the sheer originality of his form and style. He was even known to incorporate humour into his music, a notable example being the sudden loud crash at the end of his 'Surprise' Symphony, No. 94, which was included, so it is told, to wake up members of the audience who had happened to fall asleep during the performance. According to the composer himself, the quirks of his music were a consequence of the isolation he experienced working as a court musician on the castle estate of the Esterházy family.

The bulk of Haydn's composing took place within the 30-year period he was in the service of the Esterházy family, and in these days of youth there seemed little that could impede his creative output. As age slowly took hold of him, however, the musical powerhouse began to make the sobering realization that he might no longer be able to rely on body and mind as once he had.

Coming to terms with the realities of ageing can be difficult for any individual. For the musician, however, ailing health can pose the threat of stifling their creativity – their very life force. For Haydn, such challenges evidently weighed heavily on his mind when he wrote to his publishers on 12 June 1799. Now in his late sixties, Haydn complained of the mental and physical stresses which now drained his compositional faculties, and he implored those who might hear his new work to do so with understanding. Though he resisted as long as he could, ill health finally forced Haydn into retirement by 1804. He died five years later on 31 May 1809.

JOSEPH HAYDN PAINTED BY LUDWIG GUTTENBRUNN

From Joseph Haydn to his publishers, Breitkopf & Härtel, 1799

Vienna, 12 June 1799

Dearest Friend!

I am really very much ashamed to have to offend a man who has written so often and honoured me with so many marks of esteem (which I do not deserve), by answering him at this late date; it is not negligence on my part but the vast amount of <u>business</u> which is responsible, and the older I get, the more business I have to transact daily. I only regret that on account of my growing age and (unfortunately) the decrease of my mental powers, I am able to dispatch but the smallest part of it. Every day the world pays me compliments on the fire of my recent works, but no-one will believe the strain and effort it costs me to produce them: there are some days in which my enfeebled memory and the unstrung state of my nerves crush me to the earth to such an extent that I fall prey to the worst sort of depression, and thus am quite incapable of finding even a single idea for many days thereafter; until at last Providence revives me, and I can again sit down at the pianoforte and begin to scratch away again . . .

The publication of both these things does you great credit. <u>I would only wish, and hope, that the critics do not deal too severely with my Creation: they might perhaps object a little to the musical orthography of certain passages, and possibly some other minor points elsewhere; but the true connoisseur will see the reasons for them as readily as I do, and will push aside this stumbling-block. Nulla regola s[enza] e[ccezione]. N.B.: As for the tattered section in the Duet of the 'Creation', you will find it entirely different in the edition from that which Herr Traeg had the twopenny Kramer prepare for him:</u> but all this <u>underlined inter nos.</u>

Apart from all of this, I shall be very happy to serve you in any possible way. Meanwhile, my dear friend, I remain, with every esteem,

Your obliging and obedient servant,

Joseph Haydn [m.p] ria.

'I MUST RAISE STRONG OBJECTIONS TO THE LAST MOVEMENT – ONLY PLEASE DON'T TAKE IT AS A TIT-FOR-TAT ACTION'

MUSICAL GENES: FANNY AND FELIX MENDELSSOHN EXCHANGE NOTES

The differing musical fortunes of siblings Fanny (1805–47) and Felix (1809–47) Mendelssohn define the gender inequalities which dominated so much of European society in the nineteenth century. For Felix, as a man, though his parents may have been sceptical about a career in music, it was never in doubt that such a path was open to him. Despite his sister Fanny, exhibiting equal musical talents, for her a life in music was quite inconceivable.

The siblings were born into an affluent family with parents who were dedicated patrons of the arts. Their mother, Lea, was an accomplished pianist, and her musical soirées formed important social events in the calendar of Berlin's high society. She also made efforts to impart her musical knowledge to her children, and it was under her tutelage that both Fanny and Felix began their musical education.

Soon the siblings were performing alongside their mother, and all in attendance were wowed by the gifted pair. Indeed, of the two it was often Fanny who received the greatest plaudits. For her, however, social convention dictated that music could only ever be an 'ornament' in a life dictated by her duties as a mother: marriage, family and home. Such were the words of her father, Abraham, in a now famous letter sent to her when she was 15 years old in which he dismissed outright the possibility of his daughter pursuing a career as a composer beyond the home.

For the siblings, their gender-delineated fortunes were not a source of resentment, and their shared love of music served to strengthen their bond of kinship. Fanny would in fact become Felix's most trusted editor, and he posted all of his compositions on to Fanny for her critical opinion prior to their publication.

As this letter reflects, however, Fanny still longed for her own music to reach a wider audience. Moreover, there appears a lack of confidence in her own compositional abilities, a feeling fed no doubt by the barriers placed before her. Though Felix shared many of their father's reservations in this regard, he agreed to publish several of her compositions under his own name. On one occasion, when performing before Queen Victoria at Buckingham Palace in 1842, Felix had to admit that the song '*Lied Italien*', which the Queen had sung during the performance, was in truth his sister's creation.

FANNY MENDELSSOHN PAINTED BY MORITZ
DANIEL OPPENHEIM, 1842

From Fanny Mendelssohn to Felix Mendelssohn, 1835

Berlin, 17 February 1835

I want to thank you for your 2 letters and answer the appropriate items first . . . I'm ready to send off both pieces that you want, but I haven't gotten one of them back from the copyist. With respect to publishing, I wanted to ask you whether you haven't forgotten *Wer nur den lieben Gott lässt walten*, which I like very much. And if I had to choose between the 2, I would pick *Christe du Lamm Gottes*. I especially like the first movement from *Ach Gott vom*, particularly from the unison passage to the very serious and lovely entrance into A major. The aria is wonderful and beautiful, as is its text. But I must raise strong objections to the last movement – only please don't take it as a tit-for-tat action, for it certainly is not. It starts in F sharp minor and ends in a minor, or rather C major, with few modulations in between, and yet I believe the words call for an extremely constant and steadfast musical setting in the hymn. If we were together, we could easily arrive at an understanding over it, but I'm asking you to respond to this point and tell me how much your views have changed since you wrote the piece a couple of years ago.

The aria from *Wer nur den lieben Gott* reminds me to mention that many of the solo numbers in your small sacred works exhibit a trait that I wouldn't want to label a mannerism, although I don't know exactly what to call it. The style is overly simple, which I don't find natural to you – the rhythms, for example, are short and seem somewhat childlike but also somewhat childish – with the result that the music falls short of the seriousness of the genre as well as your earnest manner in treating choruses. I mainly have the aria from the Christmas music in mind, where I can easily imagine how you arrived at your setting. But the principle is applicable in many other instances. It would really be nice if we could make the selection – if it could wait until we see each other – because I'm not yet familiar enough with the music I don't possess to impart my wisdom to you.

Thanks for the tidy critique of my Quartet. Will you have it performed sometime? . . . I've composed a soprano aria that you would like better than my Quartet in terms of its form and modulations. It's rather strictly handled, and in fact I had finished it before you wrote me about the Quartet. I've reflected how I, actually not an eccentric or overly sentimental person, came to write pieces in a tender style. I believe it derives from the fact that we were young during Beethoven's last years and absorbed his style to a considerable degree. But that style is exceedingly moving and emotional. You've gone through it from start to finish and progressed beyond it in your composing, and I've remained stuck in it, not possessing the strength, however, that is necessary to sustain that tenderness. Therefore I also believe that you haven't hit upon or voiced the crucial issue. It's not so much a certain way of composing that is lacking as it is a certain approach to life, and as a result of this shortcoming, my lengthy things die in their youth of decrepitude; I lack the ability to sustain ideas properly and give them the needed consistency. Therefore lieder suit me best, in which, if need be, merely a pretty idea without much potential for development can suffice.

. . .

Do you know *Eugene Aram*? I haven't finished it yet and will give you my verdict in the next letter. Do the same and then we can see if our opinions match . . .

Adieu, my dearest – the letter has once again become chatty and long. F

. . .

'IF YOU LEAVE OUT ANY AT ALL I SHOULD PREFER IT TO BE THE A MAJOR . . . IT IS TOO REMINISCENT OF CHOPIN, AND THE BEGINNING IS TOO INSIGNIFICANT FOR BRAHMS'

CLARA SCHUMANN GIVES HER PROFESSIONAL OPINION ON JOHANNES BRAHMS' LATEST COMPOSITION

The composers Clara Schumann (1819–96) and Johannes Brahms (1833–97) shared an immutable bond almost from the moment they met. It is one that would endure for the rest of their lives, and deeply impact each of their careers.

Their first meeting occurred in 1853 when Brahms, then an aspiring 20-year-old musician, sent a formal letter of introduction to Schumann's husband Robert requesting an audience. The meeting could not have gone any better, with Robert left overawed by what he heard. Both he and his wife were adamant that they were in the presence of one of the future greats, and they both began to do all they could to support Brahms in his career.

Sadly, it would take Robert's tragic mental decline for Schumann and Brahms' friendship to truly blossom. Only four months after their first meeting, Robert Schumann attempted suicide by jumping into the Rhine River in mid-winter. He survived, but by his request was admitted thereafter to an asylum. As soon as news reached Brahms, he rushed back to Düsseldorf to do what he could to support the family of his loyal patron; Brahms became an invaluable support for Clara as she struggled to manage her grief for her husband, eight children, giving piano lessons and a musical career.

Clara had been honing her skill as a pianist from the age of four, and neither marriage nor motherhood had hindered her from becoming one of the most brilliant and sought-after Romantic recital players in Europe. She toured extensively over the course of her 61-year career, and at this difficult time Brahms stepped in to manage her affairs while she was away, including running the home and supervising her children's schooling.

Brahms stayed with Clara until Robert's death in 1856, after which they parted ways to pursue their own careers. The pair maintained a correspondence, however, that would become an important source of mentorship and emotional support for both.

Clara remained an unwavering advocate for Brahms' work, regularly playing his pieces as part of her repertoire, and even debuting ten of his works. In addition, Clara would grow to become a crucial sounding board for Brahms. Of his 122 compositions, Brahms would send 82 of them to Clara for her critical feedback. He valued her opinion over any other, and she helped refine them into the pieces we know today. In this instance, the piece Clara is reviewing is Brahms Op. 76, a piece seldom played today.

CLARA SCHUMANN TAKEN BY FRANZ HANFSTAENGL, 1857

From Clara Schumann to Johannes Brahms, 1878

Frankfort AM M., Nov. 7.

I was just about to revel in the piano pieces – I can play some of them quite well now, but most of them are terribly difficult – when your letter arrived, and so I am writing to you at once to tell you how much I am enjoying them. A great favourite of mine is the C major, and yet you want to leave it out? Why this one particularly? If you leave out any at all I should prefer it to be the A major, for although its middle movement is charming, it is too reminiscent of Chopin, and the beginning is too insignificant for Brahms – if you will excuse my saying so! In the C major piece I wish you would use the charming opening phrase again at the repeat, it would not be difficult, would it?

. . .

Would sound better with another harmony. You use such a liquid one in the following bar, and this one is so dry. I am practising the last part of the Finale hard in order to be able to play it so that it does not sound so harsh. It is rich in ideas but a little harsh after the exquisite sound of the whole. Please do not leave the piece out. It would be a pity! I like the first one in parts very much, but I cannot grow accustomed to the sudden changes of time, so that I do not enjoy it as a whole. Number two is enchanting. I also like number four, the A minor, very much. I am much in favour of the change to 3/2 time at the transition, which lengthens it a little and makes it more reposeful. I also thought of some of the alterations you have made in the F Sharp minor piece, for instance, what was . . .

[musical notation]

now goes in octaves, which sounds harsher, and it is the same the second time. Then I prefer the earlier version of the return, in which it repeats the first theme and the bass takes it up, because at the outset it does not keep on F Sharp in the bass, and that is why I was always so delighted with this earlier version. Why did you alter it? I am also very pleased with the augmentation at the return to the theme. The two short pieces in A Flat major and B Flat major are little pearls. I am in favour of repeating the first part of the A major. I think it would make the whole thing clearer. I have written more than any correspondence card would have held; but all these comments were in my mind, and possibly you may find some of them at least justified.

You must have received my parcel of proofs by now and have seen that I have set aside all scruples, and yet you will have to give my conscience credit for the fact that at least I always look through the things before sending them to you, and then leave the final decision to your judgement. As to the *Impromptus* and *Papillons*, I have begged Härtels to look for the manuscripts at Hoffmeisters. Soon I will send you the *Phantasie*.

I cannot tell you how busy I am, and in addition I have undertaken one or two private lessons (at 30 marks a time!!!) which, however, I shall have to give up, because I cannot stand working three hours in the morning; and the afternoons are impossible because there are other things to do. You see I have in any case to practise from one to two hours every day. But I have a number of charming pupils . . .

You have written to tell me how the Symphony went off at Breslau or whether you were pleased about it. If only people (like Sch . . .) would refrain from composing! It really is a pity! In this place every Tom, Dick and Harry fancies he must compose before he has even mastered harmony (but this is quite between ourselves). So farewell for to-day glad to hear what you have to say and would be interested to know your grounds for disagreeing with them.

Yours affectionately, Clara

'I SHOULD THINK IT QUITE IMPOSSIBLE TO ANSWER YOUR QUESTIONS'

EDVARD GRIEG TIRES OF HIS FAN MAIL
By 1892, Edvard Grieg had been composing music for nearly 40 years. He had worked with some of the greatest musical names in

Europe, and risen to become the most internationally renowned composer to come out of Norway. With such iconic pieces as *In the Hall of the Mountain King* (Op. 23) and the *Holberg Suite* (Op. 40) Grieg (1843–1907) captured the imagination of his listeners with romantic depictions of a mystic Nordic world, and succeeded in establishing a distinctly 'Norwegian style' of composition on an international stage.

Given his stellar résumé, one would be forgiven for assuming that Grieg – master of the Romantic style – would thus be a veritable fountain of compositional knowledge, bursting with anecdotes and experiential advice for the aspiring musician. As would become all too clear to one fan who wrote to the composer seeking to draw from this well of musical understanding, however, it seems Grieg was tight-lipped when it came to discussing the mechanics of his craft.

Grieg began his training at the Leipzig Conservatory in 1858. In his later years, he would reflect negatively on his experiences at the school, claiming that the draconian methods of the teachers meant he left the institution 'as stupid as when I entered it'. Instead, it would be the city of Leipzig itself that would leave the greatest impression on the young composer. As the heart of the German classical tradition, the city thronged with creative stimuli, and Grieg made sure to immerse himself in this cultural environment by attending every one of the orchestra rehearsals at the city concert hall.

While Leipzig may have stimulated Grieg's musical curiosities, it was back in Scandinavia in the Danish capital of Copenhagen that his sensibilities as a Romantic composer took full form. He had travelled to the city following his graduation from the Leipzig Conservatory in 1863, and over the next three years he met many of the leading figures in the Scandinavian folk music movement. One of the most influential meetings was that with the composer and fellow Norwegian Rikard Nordraak. Nordraak was the foremost figure in the nationalist movement in Norwegian music, and he was set on distilling the unique qualities of his homeland into musical form (an ideology captured in the piece '*Ja, vi elsker dette landet*', now the national anthem of Norway). He compelled Grieg to explore his Norwegian identity in his music, and stirred in him a creative impulse that would define the rest of his career.

To recount this winding road of compositional development would have required time and effort Grieg clearly did not have when responding to this particular fan. It may be that Grieg struggled to render his art into words, or it may be that he simply did not wish to.

EDVARD GRIEG

From Edvard Grieg to a fan, 1892

Bergen, Norway

June 29, 1892

Dear Sir!

I should think it quite impossible to answer your questions

1) as I have no method at all when composing!
2) as the art of composition is not at all to be learned and still – <u>must</u> be learned!
3) As I have no particular favourite composer. All good composers are my favourites!

Yours faithfully

Edvard Grieg

Bergen, Norway
June 29, 1872

Dear Sir!

        I should think
it quite impossible to
answer your questions
1) as I have no method
at all when composing!
2) as the art of compo-
sition is not at all to
be learned and still —
<u>must</u> be learned!
3) as I have no par-
ticular favorite composer.
All good composers

'THE HOUR OF MY THIRTY-FIRST YEAR HAS STRUCK AND
I STILL AM NOT VERY SURE OF MY AESTHETIC AND THERE
ARE STILL THINGS I DO NOT KNOW! (HOW TO WRITE
MASTERPIECES, FOR EXAMPLE)'

CLAUDE DEBUSSY'S SELF-DOUBTS

There are a multitude of ways people cope with ageing. Some
celebrate each birthday with fervour and style, while others let
their birthday pass by with little fanfare, utterly indifferent to the
transitions between youth, adulthood and old age. Then there are
those of us who feel the passing of time as a crushing vice on their
dreams, or as sand through an hourglass, rapidly slipping away.
The French composer Claude Debussy certainly found himself in
this last group in 1893, when the passing of his 31st birthday left
him questioning not only his creative abilities but also his overall
existence.

Debussy (1862–1918) was an expert in creating original
harmonies and musical structures that contributed to some of the
most widely recognizable music, such as *Clair de lune* ('Moonlight',
1905) in *Suite bergamasque*, and *La Mer* ('The Sea', 1905). Before
these successes, however, Debussy grappled with uncertainty about
his creative abilities that led to spiralling introspection.

When the dust settled on his birthday celebrations, Debussy
wrote to his friend and fellow composer Ernest Chausson of his
melancholic reflections on his artistic journey thus far, relating to
the Gothic woe of Edgar Allen Poe's stories. The letter captures
Debussy's struggle between his grand aspirations and crushing self-
doubt, expressed through vivid imagery and lyrical language. He
shares a recent encounter with Henri de Régnier, blending humour
and introspection as he navigated the complexities of friendship
and artistic discourse. Debussy's musings on music's accessibility
reveal his longing for a more profound connection to the art form,
advocating for a 'Society of Esoteric Music' that would elevate its
symbolic qualities beyond the reach of the masses.

Amid his reflections, Debussy expresses a yearning for companionship, lamenting the absence of Chausson, and the fear of creating in isolation. This correspondence not only sheds light on Debussy's artistic struggles but also highlights the intimate bond between two composers navigating the challenges of their craft. Through his eloquent prose, Debussy invited Chausson into his world, seeking solace and understanding in the shared experience of artistry.

From Claude Debussy to Ernest Chausson, 1893

[Paris] September 6, 1893

Dear Friend:

I've tried in vain, I can't succeed in brightening up the sadness of my landscape – sometimes my days are as dark and gloomy and silent as those of an Edgar Allan Poe hero, and thus my romantic soul like a ballad by Chopin! Too many memories fill my solitude, but I can't throw them away, well, one must live and wait. It remains to be seen whether I haven't got a wrong number for the bus of Happiness, though I'd be quite content with standing room! (Excuse this cheap philosophy!)

Now the hour of my thirty-first year has struck and I still am not very sure of my aesthetic and there are still things I do not know! (how to write masterpieces, for example, and then how to be very serious, among other things having the weakness of caring too much about my life and never seeing its realities until they become insurmountable). Perhaps I'm more to be pitied than condemned; anyway, while writing you, I'm counting on your forgiveness and patience.

I had a visit from Henri de Régnier, who shows great liking for you – it's somewhat like speaking of hemp in the house of one who has been hanged! Also, to make things worse, I made myself as charming as possible and played *L'Après-midi d'un faune,* which he found as hot as a furnace and he praised the shivering in it! (Make what you can of this.) On the other hand, when he talks poetry, he is extremely interesting and shows very refined sensibilities.

While he was speaking to me about certain words in the French language whose gold had become tarnished through too much use by the *hoi polloi*, I thought to myself that the same thing was true of certain chords whose sound had become commonplace in music for export; this reflection is not strikingly novel unless I add that at the same time they have lost their symbolic quality. Really, music should have been a hermetic science, protected by texts so long and difficult to interpret that they surely would have discouraged the herd of people who use it as casually as they do a handkerchief! Moreover, instead of trying to extend art further among the people, I propose the establishment of a 'Society of Esoteric Music' and you'll see that neither M. Helmann nor M. de Bonnières will belong. While I am writing to you, the girl at the piano below me is sawing out some music in D which is really fearful! Alas, it's living proof that I'm right.

And you, my dear friend, are you working hard, are you feeling content? Haven't you any more pretty little children who create an uproar like 500,000 claps of thunder! Have you definitely decided to let that poor Genievre die! The last thing you showed me led me to expect very lovely music from you – I'm waiting with great confidence. Me, I'm working like mad, but it is my misanthropic existence – anyway I'm not pleased with what I'm doing. I wish you were here for a while. I'm afraid of working in a vacuum and it begins to seem like youthful barbarism, which in any case, I can't resist.

Your poor Claude Achille is waiting like another Sister Anne for your return, which will fill his heart with joy. I embrace you affectionately.

Claude Debussy

'DOGS BARK AND HOWL, THE COWS COMING IN FROM THE FIELDS MOO AND RUN IN ALL DIRECTIONS'

SERGEI PROKOFIEV DAMNS THE GRAMOPHONE

In 1904, Sergei Prokofiev arrived at the St Petersburg Conservatory as a musical prodigy. Despite being only 13 years of age, the teenager so impressed the examiners at his entrance interview that they saw fit to permit him immediate entry into the prestigious institution. Prokofiev (1891–1953) had been set on pursuing a musical career ever since the first time he had watched his mother play the piano in their family home; gaining a formal education at the prestigious Conservatory was the crucial next step in fulfilling this dream. For all his promise, however, it soon became apparent to those in charge of the conservatory that the 'prodigal child' might have been better suited to the title 'problem child'.

Prokofiev later described his time at the St Petersburg Conservatory as one of 'deep disappointment'. As a budding modernist, he was eager to push the boundaries of conventional styles of composition. Such radical ideas were not well received by Prokofiev's teachers, however, and they were unwilling to accommodate his idiosyncrasies.

For his teachers, Prokofiev's youthful confidence came across as petulant and egotistical. For his fellow students too, having such a precocious minor studying alongside them became irksome, particularly when Prokofiev developed the habit of keeping tabs on the mistakes his classmates had made during lessons.

Underneath his bravado, however, remained a vulnerability that Prokofiev could not deny. In 1909, having just graduated from the Conservatory, he wrote to his fellow classmate Vera Alpers from his hometown of Sontsivka in rural Ukraine. Among his various complaints he gave insight into his process of composition, including the local nuisances which he found disrupted his musical flow. In addition, he expressed his anxieties concerning the debuting of a recent composition. Likening the experience to that of maternal protectiveness, Prokofiev feared for how it would be received publicly – fears that would prove well founded. In 1913, on the premiere of his second piano concerto, for instance, one critic described it as 'a babel of insane sounds heaped upon one another without rhyme or reason'.

While unsettling for most popular audiences, Prokofiev's pioneering style found a willing audience among the modernists, and he is now widely held to be one of the most influential musical figures of the twentieth century. Ballet was a medium in which he proved particularly successful and, though certainly not his most ambitious piece, perhaps the best known today is his ballet *Peter and the Wolf* (1936), which he composed in an effort to encourage children to take an interest in classical music.

SERGEI PROKOFIEV AT HIS PIANO, C. 1918–20

From Sergei Prokofiev to Vera Alpers, 1909

26th July, 1909

Sontsovka

You haven't written me for so long, dear Vera Vladimirovna, that I'm beside myself with despair. But in fact you should be acting nicely towards me, and here's why. Honored Avraam Isakovich Kankarovich, after arguing with his impresario, proceeded perpendicularly and left Voronezh, and I, with my charming sinfonietta, ended up like a beached whale stranded on the shore. So this damn Kankaroshka, whom I had always considered a wimpy milksop, suddenly took it into his head to behave decisively, just when it wasn't appropriate. Isn't that a joke, or what? When autumn comes I'll have to get down to serious work and get it played in Petersburg. True, they'll perform it better than they would have in Voronezh, but there will also be a lot of arranging to do. In short, every autumn I feel like an anxious *mamashenka* with a grown-up daughter who has to be groomed and introduced to society.

Kankaroshka's news got me terribly upset, but it didn't spoil my mood. Lately, I've had to go through so much with the creation of my sinfonietta that I was really happy to be liberated from the obligation to push it any further. Now I'm composing a little at a time, gradually, and in the meantime I'm writing études for Winkler and a mazurka in which both hands play around in parallel fourths.

'Oh, you dear daughter! How did they end up letting you go to your deep blue sea?' (Actually, it's probably more like gray.) I, too, am planning to exhibit some filial tenderness and visit my mamenka, who has been in Essentuki for two weeks already in treatment for her rheumatism. Only I'm not going to the sea but the mountains, the tall, snow-covered mountains! The three pounds I lost with God's good graces I have put back on, but now I'll probably lose them again. What can you do . . . After all, you don't waste away living in the country!

Along with your letter I received one from your namesake (who has already managed to make up with me and even to expend a lot of film taking pictures of me). I'm sending you a shot she took following my instructions, setting up two cameras at the same time – one from the front and one from the back. Then they were pasted together. What resulted was a sort of doll. It doesn't look at all like me, but at first glance the shots and I do have something inexplicable in common.

Not long ago civilization sprang up in our backwoods in the form of a gramophone bought by one of the peasant men. And now towards evening, this damned invention stands outdoors in front of his hut and starts to wheeze its horrible songs. The crowd that gathers makes a racket, expressing its joy, and pretends to sing along. Dogs bark and howl, the cows coming in from the fields moo and run in all directions, and, to top off all this torture, someone from a neighbouring hut starts to play along on the accordion, off-key. At first I try closing all the windows, then I sit down at the piano, but finally I lose my patience and go off riding on my bicycle in the fields so as to spare myself this frightful cacophony.

Write, Verochka, adio –

Prokofiev

'MUSIC IS SOME KIND OF ELECTRICITY THAT MAKES A RADIO OUT OF A MAN AND HIS DIAL IS IN HIS HEAD AND HE JUST SINGS ACCORDING TO HOW HE'S A FEELING'

WOODY GUTHRIE SHARES THE SECRETS TO WRITING THE PERFECT FOLK SONG

Few musicians surpass Woody Guthrie in their influence on the musical landscape of twentieth-century America. With such songs as 'This Land is Your Land' and 'Do Re Mi', as well as hundreds of others written over the course of the 1930s and 1940s, Guthrie (1912–67) managed to cut to the heart of the American rural experience, and establish a legacy which has served to inspire a whole generation of future greats, including Bob Dylan, Bruce Springsteen and Johnny Cash.

Guthrie famously wrote more than 3,000 songs over the course of his career – a number so unfathomably impressive that it has naturally prompted many to question how he was able to maintain such staggering momentum in his writing. Fortunately, this is a question that Guthrie himself answered in a letter written to the musicologist Alan Lomax in 1940.

Folk songs, Guthrie wrote, could have their roots in any number of scenarios and experiences. Many of the artist's songs were inspired by his own experiences of growing up during a particularly difficult period for the rural Mid-West. Guthrie, who was born in Okemah, Oklahoma, witnessed first-hand the strife and upheaval of the Dust Bowl, an ecological phenomenon caused by severe droughts and improper farming that turned prairie land into dusty wastelands, causing economic hardship and a mass migration of people. Guthrie became one of these migrants, leaving his home to travel across the country to find work in California. He channelled his experiences into his album *Dust Bowl Ballads*, which earned him the title the 'Dust Bowl Troubadour'.

Reading his letter to Lomax, it is obvious that there was one overriding principle, reaching beyond his Oklahoma roots, that dictated Guthrie's mantra and method for composition: his music had to reflect the everyday experiences of the common people. Guthrie's songs combined simple, poignant lyrics with catchy melodies; he also frequently adapted existing tunes, allowing for a fluid interplay between music and message.

Above all, Guthrie's music demonstrates respect for his audiences, and it was this respect that helped him become the voice for people experiencing extensive social and economic change, connecting with audiences both within the United States and beyond even today.

WOODY GUTHRIE WITH SINGER MARGARET JOHNSON FOR A
RADIO PERFORMANCE, 1940

From Woody Guthrie to Alan Lomax, 1940

September 19, 1940

Dear Alan

Just thought I'd write you a few more lines tonight on as many
different subjects as I can get down in one line. Mainly about a few
thoughts that I been thinking about making up songs and stuff like
that . . . I think one mistake some folks make in trying to write songs
that will interest folks is to try to cover too much territory or to

make it too much of a sermon. A folk song ought to be pretty well
satisfied just to tell the facts and let it go at that. You hadn't ought
to try to be too funny because if you just tell folks the truth they'll
laugh at every other word. The best of all funny songs have got a
mighty sincere backbone. These are the old deathbed and graveyard
and parted lover songs that I sing more than any others when I need
to cheer myself up . . . People that laugh at songs laugh because it
made them think of something and they want you to leave a good
bit up to their guesswork and imagination and it takes on a friendly
and warm atmosphere like you was thanking them for being good
listeners and giving them credit for being able to guess the biggest
part of the meaning. Lots of songs I make up when Im [sic] laughing
and celebrating make folks cry and songs I make up when Im [sic]
feeling down and out makes people laugh. These two upside down
feelings has got to be in any song to make it take a hold and last.

Usually I set down and knock off a song in about 30 minutes or
a hour but in most of them I've been going around humming and
whistling it and a trying to get it all straight in my head what I want
to say and why I want to say it and usually when I decide just exactly
who the song is a going to help out if it's the right bunch I can really
beat or scribble her down in a hurry. The reason why you want to
write songs is what keeps you going. If you got enough reason to
write I say that you can knock off two or 3 pretty fair songs a week
and a pretty dam [sic] good one over the week end . . . The main thing
is to set your head on some subject you want to harp on and haul
off and start and you can write 25 or 30 or 500 songs on the same
subject if your subject is a helping people. I took as my subject songs
that would make people want to help people, and I am now on my
202th — two oh tooth. I've wrote up songs and tore them up. I bet I
tore up more than a orchestra feller could shake a stick at. And lots
of folks are making up songs all of the time and they dont [sic] know it.
I hear so many people coming around me and going on about where
you get your words and your tunes. Well I get my words and tunes off
of the hungry folks and they get the credit for all I pause to scribble

down. I feel a little bit guilty for not taking more time out to jot down more. As you know I aint [*sic*] able to read no music note I just get the time to grinding through my head and jot the music down on my old guitar. You know pretty near it everybody is a making up all kinds of tunes all along but they just dont [*sic*] know about it . . .

Everybody makes up music and some folks try to harness it and put it to work just like steam that you caint [*sic*] hold in your hand or vitamens [*sic*] you hear the doctor charge you three dollars to describe or electricity that makes big engines run and great big wheels go around. If it would of been left up to me I'd of been too busy trapseing [*sic*] around over the country and making a guitar sound like a freight train to of stopped long enough to catch electricity and make it help you but of course Mr Edison had some men working for him and tonight I'm a writing this by a light, a floor lamp with three shifts forwards and a radio with 3 backwards and I've got the light and the other folks can have the music. Music is some kind of electricity that makes a radio out of a man and his dial is in his head and he just sings according to how he's a feeling . . .

A folk song is whats [*sic*] wrong and how to fix it, or it could be whose [*sic*] hungry and where their mouth is, or whose [*sic*] out of work and where the job is, or whose [*sic*] broke and where the money is, or whose [*sic*] carrying a gun and where the peace is . . .

All I know how to do Alan is to just keep a plowing right on down the avenue watching what I can see and listening to what I can hear and trying to learn about everybody I meet every day and try to make one part of the country feel like they know the other part and one end of it help the other end – cause if a horse fly is dealing a horse trouble on the left nose hole, it's the tail that swishes and drives the fly off.

Take it Easy but take it

Woody Guthrie

Sept 19th 1940
New York Town

'IF I HAVEN'T GOT SHINGLES, IT'S NOT FROM WANT OF TRYING'

MICHAEL TIPPETT ON HIS WRITING-INDUCED FATIGUE

Few other letters give such rich insight into the experience of being a musician than those of Michael Tippett. A superbly articulate writer, he discusses his creative process quite openly and often in his correspondence, and expresses the multiplicity of emotion he experienced along the way. Much of this is found in the letters he shared with fellow composers, and one of the most fruitful and creatively charged connections was with Benjamin Britten.

Their correspondence reveals not only their deep mutual respect and admiration for one another, but also their contrasting approaches to composition. Tippett, known for his innovative and complex musical language, often grappled with the psychological and emotional depths of his work, as evidenced in this letter to Britten. Describing his current project, the opera *The Midsummer Marriage*, Tippett emphasized its prolonged creative process and the fatigue that stemmed from his intense focus on crafting such a profound artistic statement. Tippett's tendency to draw from a wide array of influences, including visual and theatrical elements, showcases his ambition to simplify his music into an accessible yet richly textured experience, despite the challenges he faced.

On the other hand, Britten's compositional style is characterized by clarity and lyricism, often rooted in traditional forms while infusing modern sensibilities. Tippett's longing for Britten's 'wonderful ease of composition' highlights the contrast in their methods – Tippett's intricate, sometimes burdensome inventive process compared to Britten's more fluid and intuitive approach. As they engaged in discussions about each other's works and aspirations, including the optimistic prospect of a collaboration or performance, their dialogue underscored the evolution of contemporary opera and song within the English musical landscape. Their shared experiences shaped their artistic identities, ultimately leading to a rich tapestry of collaboration that reflects their individual artistry while contributing to a vibrant musical community. In this correspondence, Tippett's heartfelt musings become a lens through which to explore the interplay of innovation and tradition that defines both composers' legacies.

A YOUNG MICHAEL TIPPETT POSES FOR A PHOTOGRAPH, 1930S

From Michael Tippett to Benjamin Britten, 1950

3 March 1950

My dear Ben,

[. . .] I've heard a lot about *Billy Budd* and know you are just starting. I shall be finishing about the same time as you or a trifle later. The *Midsummer Marriage* will however wait till 52 before it leaps into the fray. I think [Eric] Walter White has some hopes that if the plans for *Billy Budd* mature and are a success, the good folk there might risk another English presentation.

I am just about to send Act I off to the printer (vocal score). Act 2 is all but finished. It's a kind of prolonged [Prélude á L'] Après-midi d'un faune. Act 2 is not as long as Act I is so won't take such an age – but it's got some tremendous moments in it.

I find I suffer now from a deep-seated fatigue that's always round the corner, waiting to pounce. I have never kept so long at one huge continuous invention. It isn't complicated. I don't seem to use anything but common chords. And there's no counterpoint!! Though that will not prevent Howes (under whose skin any music of mine invariably gets) dismissing it as polyphonic. I sigh all the time for your wonderful ease of composition, and what I can steal I do. But it's less than I hoped! Though there's a lovely phrase from [*Albert*] *Herring* (not my favourite of your works as you know) which I've got into the most splendid aria I've written yet – for the heroine, Jenifer. But in fact I've never (since the *Child*) been so cursed by a work, which seems to live me, with all its stage trappings into the bargain. I've had to become extremely visual in composition. It probably wouldn't have take [*sic*] so long if I weren't venturing into such a new group and risking such a lot. I have to shake down such a mass of material of all sorts in order to come at a truly simplified image, that it seems to require hours of labour and forcing merely brings a crisis of fatigue. If I haven't got shingles, it's not from want of trying. Poor old Peter. But he really must take it easier.

I want to do some songs if I can and fancy [having] at some poems, which I'm wanting to see. But I don't want to write second-rate stuff for you.

I'm very happy and cheerful, though I get depressive moments due to this so unexpectedly long wait – I imagined it would have been quicker. But there's been no stoppage, only a continuous high pressure of creation. It ought to be good one feels after all that. And that scares me a bit. There's some lovely music for tenor incidentally. A gay and spring-like love song at the very start of Act I. And a rather bigger 'Dionysian' aria later in the act, after the hero has been 'below', in the catholic world.

It's just typical of my life that I can't even write you a letter without pouring out words about the opera. It's a kind of monomania. I'd love to see you. But I guess you're going to be shut up with Billy Budd. Should I though come and visit you? Or make a date in town?

Give my love to Peter, and my regards to [E. M.] Forster.

herzlichst

Michael

'WHEN I SING I HAVE TO STAND IN THE MIDDLE OF THE STUDIO WITH EARPHONES ON, AND EVERYONE ELSE WATCHES FROM THE OTHER ROOM'

SYD BARRETT REPORTS FROM THE RECORDING STUDIO

Over the last 70 years or so, many recording studios have become iconic landmarks, owing to the famous musicians who have worked and produced their most popular songs there. Abbey Road Studios in London, for instance, has become an important place of pilgrimage for any true Beatles fan, with over 100,000 people reportedly flocking to the location every year. In the United States, Sun Studio in Memphis shares a similar reputation as a hub of musical innovation, famed nowadays as the musical birthplace for such legendary figures as Elvis Presley, Jerry Lee Lewis and Johnny Cash.

For the musician, these often small, enclosed spaces full of amps, microphones and countless wires can effectively become a second home, as they spend hours, weeks and months locked away trying to capture the perfect recording of the tracks they have worked so hard to compose. It is, therefore, often a highly private sphere for the musician, acting as a place in which they can remove themselves from the world and focus solely on their music. Luckily, we get a glimpse into this hidden world through a letter sent by the enigmatic frontman of Pink Floyd, Roger 'Syd' Barrett (1946–2006) to his lifelong friend and former girlfriend, Jenny.

When the words 'prog rock' are mentioned, one of the first bands that spring to mind is Pink Floyd. Their albums *The Dark Side of the Moon* (1973), *Wish You Were Here* (1975) and *The Wall* (1979) have come to define the 1970s, and are still celebrated as some of the finest records produced by any British rock group. (The first two were also recorded at Abbey Road.) In 1965, however, the band was still just a fledgling group of musicians trying to find their feet among the variety of new psychedelic sounds reverberating around Britain at the time. They had come to the studio to record several pieces, the majority of which were Barrett's personal compositions.

Barrett was the original frontman of Pink Floyd, performing as their singer, guitarist and primary songwriter until 1968. Under his stylistic guidance, the band landed two hit singles ('Arnold Layne' and 'See Emily Play'), and their debut album *The Piper at the Gates of Dawn* (of which Barrett wrote all but three songs) received widespread acclaim. Crucial to their success was Barrett's innovations in producing a free, psychedelic sound in his compositions. He became known for his eerie, echoing style of guitar playing, and was one of the first British rock musicians to sing with a distinctly English accent. His lyric writing was also highly applauded for its magical and whimsical tone which encapsulated the artistic trends within pop music of the late 1960s.

As we read the letter, we see a sense of excitement at the opportunity to finally make tangible the music they have been playing. Equally, however, it seems the studio was not an environment Barrett felt entirely comfortable in.

Sadly, Barrett would not be able to share in Pink Floyd's eventual success, as mental illness fed by the taking of hallucinogenic drugs made Barrett a disruptive force in the band. Nevertheless, he remains of endless interest to fans for his idiosyncratic role in Pink Floyd's development.

PINK FLOYD, FROM LEFT: RICHARD WRIGHT, ROGER WATERS, NICK MASON, SYD BARRETT, 1960S

From Syd Barrett to Jen, 1965

Dear Jen, you are a little dish.

I'll tell you everything that happened at the recording. We took all the gear into the studio which was lit by horrid white lights, and covered with wires and microphones. Rog had his amp behind a screen and Nicki was also screened off, and after a little bit of chat we tested everything for balance, and then recorded five numbers more or less straight off; but only the guitars and drums. We're going to add all the singing and piano etc. next Wednesday. The tracks sound terrific so far, especially King Bee.

When I sing I have to stand in the middle of the studio with earphones on, and everyone else watches from the other room, and I cant [sic] see them at all but they can all see me. Also I can only just hear what I'm singing.

I hope you got home alright Jen, and that you had a good time. You wouldn't have been able to come in to the recording and anyway it went on till after midnight, and would have been a whopping drag for you.

It was a nice thing to be which was tra tra la. (do not bother to interupt [sic])

Do what you want Jen. I love you very much and want to hear from you and you are very pretty.

I am a bit fed up with everything today and I want to be in Cambridge or Greece but not in London where all I do is spend money and travel. The sun is shining though.

Love Roger

'LYRIC IDEAS ARE AS ILLUSIVE [SIC] AS FIREFLIES . . . THE MOMENT YOU GIVE THEM YOUR ATTENTION, THEY ARE GONE'

NICK CAVE ON SONGWRITING

'I feel the process is like trying to describe something which I can only see imperfectly, or out of the corner of my eye . . . Did you ever experience that?' one fan, identified simply as 'S', wrote to the Australian musician Nick Cave in 2018, enquiring about his songwriting process. In fact, the enquiry could not be better placed, as Cave (b. 1957) has received multiple accolades for his songwriting and work as frontman with the rock band Nick Cave and the Bad Seeds, whose hits include 'O Children', 'Red Right Hand' and 'Into My Arms', among many more.

Cave's early foray into songwriting featured lyrics circling the themes of the Old Testament, dripping with imagery of sin and damnation, which fitted the dark aesthetic and raucous performances of his post-punk band the Birthday Party. The group disbanded shortly after moving to West Berlin in the early 1980s, and both Cave and Michael Harvey began a new project back in Melbourne with a rockier sound. As the Bad Seeds, Cave and his band have produced 18 studio albums from 1984 to 2024 – a mammoth discography traversing 40 years of its members' lives: their loves, losses and everything in between.

While some musicians are secretive about how they put these experiences into words, Cave responded to 'S's' enquiry with a refreshing frankness: songwriting, it seems, is a collaboration between the artist and this mysterious 'other' lurking just beyond reach – a flickering emotion or concept waiting to be unleashed by the artist through their open heart and mind. It is perhaps this openness to whatever may be thrown in his creative path that has made Cave such a prolific and decorated songwriter.

From Nick Cave to 'S', 2018

Dear S.,

I very much like your description of the creative process – to see something imperfectly or out of the corner of your eye. This is exactly right. A good song idea never fronts up to you, never looks you in the eye, never announces itself – at least not in my experience. Lyric ideas are as illusive [*sic*] as fireflies. They are spirits flitting between the trees. The moment you give them your attention, they are gone.

But still you write, because over the years you have learned – midst the nonsensical hieroglyphics you compulsively scrawl in your notebooks, the dumb single lines that stare contemptuously back at you, the song titles that excite you then lose their magic the next time you look at them, the half-baked and derivative ideas, the stolen lines, the Freudian doodles, the desperate over-egged metaphors and lunatic, pencil-snapping, last-ditch attempts at something, my God, *anything* – you have learned to hold fast and trust. You have learned from hard-won experience that within this pile of words something mysterious is going on, something beyond the reaches of your understanding, something that simply takes its own sweet time and of which you are a tiny part – you are the guy who turns up to hold the pencil – and that suddenly, without warning, you find you have taken one line of no consequence and attached it to another line of no consequence and a kind of reverberation begins between the two lines, a throbbing – or as I like to call it, a 'shimmering' – it is something you can actually see! And as the two combined lines pulsate, they begin to collect significance impossibly, and at a rapid rate, to load up with meaning, even to call down a melody, and your heart begins to beat as if for the first time in God knows how long, and you come alive, you become an actual person, a functional, competent human being deserving of their place on this earth, because you know, suddenly, more than anything, that you are on to something and this shimmering convergence of words is setting off on its journey to change the world.

As for *Fireflies*, we are still searching for it.

Much love, Nick

CHAPTER FIVE

PERFORMANCE

With 'performance' we arrive at the heart of the matter. Or do we? Well, it rather depends on who you ask. Arnold Schoenberg once allegedly observed that 'the performer, for all his intolerable arrogance, is totally unnecessary except as his interpretations make the music understandable to an audience unfortunate enough not to be able to read it in print.' Some might go further and suggest that even the idea of 'interpretation' affords the performer too much agency, and that their job, as Stravinsky put it, should simply be to 'execute' the music: to convert it from score to sound precisely as directed by the composer.

The moment, sometime in the first millennium AD, when music began to be written down, saw the beginnings of a subtle shift in the understanding of it which, taken to extremes, ends with Schoenberg's damning of the performer. Around that time, awareness began to develop of a piece of music as existing independently of its performance. This might seem obvious, but before it was written down – codified – music was performed from memory and possessed an improvisatory quality. Or at least, as musical ideas were handed down through the generations they grew and changed, almost like an organism: there was no real sense of a specific and definite 'work', and consequently no real sense of one 'performance' of a piece that could be compared to another. When music began to be written down, the idea of a *piece* – a set of melodies and harmonies performed in a certain order with a beginning, a middle and an end – became (slowly) the dominant Western way of thinking about music. This allowed for musical works of great and increasing complexity, as well as works that placed great and increasing demands on those performing them. As such, those performing musical works became specialists, sought after for their skills and remunerated accordingly. The line is not a particularly wiggly one between this and the star performers of today.

It's a hard sell today to claim that the performer is, as Schoenberg put it, 'totally unnecessary' (although technological advances may yet come to prove him right.) He may have been closer to the mark with the accusation of 'intolerable arrogance', but then again maybe not – while it is possible to read some of the letters in this chapter and see on their surface a sheen of arrogance, this is often, it seems, a thin veiling of vulnerability.

If 'performance' is anything at all it is surely the making vulnerable of oneself. Vulnerable in the moment: utter concentration on the act of creating at the expense of everything else; and vulnerable in a deeper sense: a presenting to the world of the culmination of a lifetime's work, the very best of oneself offered up for appreciation – but also for criticism. The criticism of a performance is, for a musician, dangerously close to the criticism of their very being – their personhood – and therefore goes very deep indeed. We see a level-headed Giuseppe Verdi enjoying the absurdity of receiving a bill – which, extraordinarily, he pays – from an audience member dissatisfied by his new opera *Aida* ('Theatre 8.oo lire. Disgustingly bad dinner at the station 2.o').

We must be honest, though: a 1-star review is almost always more fun to read than a 3- or 4-star review. 'Cataclysmically awful' is going to win out over 'fairly good' every time. But 5-star reviews are also fun to read, especially if, as in the case of the two letters in this chapter that might fall into that category, those 5-star reviews have been written by the performers or composers themselves. Should we expect modesty from a young Mozart, or from Enrico Caruso after his Milan debut? It would be foolish to, and we can hardly begrudge the 18-year-old Mozart his success, especially as the important things are not neglected in his letter ('1,000 kisses to Miss Bimberl [the dog]')], or indeed Caruso, whose letter, while evidently written on a triumphant high, is shot through with love and affection for its recipient.

This is, after all, then, the 'heart of the matter', for without performance all we have in music is an idea; an exercise; a concept. But to read this chapter is perhaps to be reminded that, as much as performances are increasingly commodities to be bought and sold, at their heart are people: people whose love for music is such that they have no choice but to make themselves publicly and entirely vulnerable for our enjoyment. That is a remarkable thing.

'THE SINGERS ARE A LOT OF OLD CROCKS'

A SECOND-RATE PERFORMANCE OF A FIRST-RATE OPERA: GIACOMO PUCCINI DESPAIRS AT THE REHEARSALS FOR LE VILLI

It is no mean feat to bring a musical performance to the stage. It is an operation which involves managing a variety of moving parts, of which the music is, albeit an integral one, only one small part. Be it an opera, then a fitting librettist must be sought. Be it a ballet, then a choreographer capable of rendering the music into physical expression. For the music, an orchestra of accomplished musicians must be assembled, along with a conductor sympathetic to the composer's style. Then there is the cast, preferably of the highest order. Finally, a stage manager to bring the production to life.

To make sure these cogs are moving in rhythm on the opening night is what dictates the success or downfall of a composer's creation, no matter how good their work might be. There is, consequently, a huge amount of faith placed by the composer in those who interpret their music, and bring to life that which exists in their mind's eye. We can only imagine Giacomo Puccini's frustration, therefore, when he made a visit to the theatre to check on the developing preparations for the 1884 Turin premiere of his debut ballet-opera Le Villi.

The production was Puccini's (1858–1924) first stage work, and it had already enjoyed a successful debut in Milan on 31 May that year. Now *Le Villi* was being brought to the city of Turin, and Puccini was eager to maintain this momentum. These aspirations were soon scuppered after he attended one of the rehearsals; much to his dismay, what *could* go wrong *had* gone wrong.

Incensed, Puccini picked up his pen to air his frustrations to the music publisher Giulio Ricordi. Ricordi was a close friend of Puccini, and had in fact written to him to hear how preparations were going. In response, both Puccini and his librettist Ferdinando Fontana gave a no-holds-barred report.

Thankfully, Fontana's optimism as to the eventual success of the production won through, and the ballet closed to great applause on 26 December.

GIACOMO PUCCINI, 1908

From Giacomo Puccini and Ferdinando Fontana to Giulio Ricordi, 1884

Dear Signor Giulio,

We thank you very much for your most kind telegram. We had intended to write to you yesterday, as we had promised, but decided to wait till we were able to give you definite news.

There is no doubt that the performance of *Le Villi* at the Regio will be not only very far from what we wished, but also very inferior to that which it could have been in a first-class theatre.

The singers are a lot of old crocks. The orchestra is weak and lifeless, and even the baton of the valiant Bolzoni is powerless to infuse any sport into it. What with being new to the orchestra, and because he is a little cold of temperament, he has not yet succeeded – and tonight is the full rehearsal – in making it go as Puccini wants it. I may add that Puccini, who is really very patient in his criticisms, does not dare to make any more, because the only suggestion which he made last night was received with scant courtesy.

The choruses are lamentably weak. At times they are simply not heard. And you know that the acoustic properties of the Regio are of the worst.

I say nothing of the staging. We have not yet been allowed to see the scenery!

Puccini has little hope. I, on the other hand, believe in spite of everything that it will be a success. The first act is safe. The second will not in its beginning have the effect it should have, but the music is beautiful, and it will have more success as it goes on if the cast and orchestra learn anything from practice.

The less said about the ballet music the better. They have foisted a third-rate dancer on us as ballet master.

After tonight's rehearsal we shall send you further news. What troubles us more than anything else in all this is that we should in your eyes be cutting the same figure as all the rest of the miserable composers who, the stupider they are themselves, complain the more about everything and everybody. But you have asked for information and here it is, and perfectly true. And, besides, you know us, and we believe that you will not lump us with them . . . ; especially as, notwithstanding the justifiable fears of Puccini, I, fortified by my own feeling and the admiring comments which everybody in the theatre is making about the work of the popular young musician, persist in believing that we shall have a great and real success, in spite of everything.

But at the Scala the preparations will have to be much more careful, because there they do things seriously. With the manager here, for instance, who refused to give Puccini even one extra instrument, it is possible to compromise, but at Milan it would be impossible. Our greetings to you and Signor Tornaghi and regards to your family,

D. F. Fontana
G. Puccini

'THE OPERA CONTAINS ABSOLUTELY NOTHING THRILLING OR ELECTRIFYING... IT WILL FILL THE THEATRE A FEW MORE TIMES AND THEN GATHER DUST IN THE ARCHIVES'

GIUSEPPE VERDI'S DISSATISFIED CUSTOMER

On Christmas Eve 1871, Giuseppe Verdi's *Aida* debuted in Cairo. A blistering, tragic love story about the relationship between an Egyptian warrior and an enslaved Ethiopian princess set in the Old Kingdom, *Aida* was a breathtaking production to behold, and became an instant success with audiences all over the world.

After the dazzling debut in Egypt, Verdi's (1813–1901) 24th opera opened in Milan in early 1872, and spread to the remainder of Italy's finest opera houses, including the Teatro Regio di Parma on 20 April that year. It was here that, among the raucous applause of hundreds, one man remained sat in his seat, entirely unimpressed by the performance he had just witnessed.

Indeed, the gentleman in question, Prospero Bertani, found the opera so underwhelming that he decided to visit the theatre for a second time, determined to discover what exactly everybody else seemed to think was so magnificent about Verdi's latest masterpiece. Once again Bertani left the theatre disappointed, his dissatisfaction this time compounded by the fact that he had now made two separate trips to Parma to see it. Determined to rectify the situation, Bertani wrote to the composer himself to request a refund.

One can only speculate how Verdi reacted when he received Bertani's letter – a note that not only outlined his every disappointment in Verdi's new opera, but also provided an invoice for reimbursement for the performances and a 'disgustingly bad dinner' the patron ate at the station. Perhaps he threw back his head and laughed, or perhaps he exploded in an angry spew of insults. Either way, when Verdi eventually picked up his pen to respond to the audacious request he managed to see the humour in it, and instructed his publisher, Giulio Ricordi, to honour the requested refunds – at least in part. As far as he was concerned, he bore no responsibility for the quality of Bertani's dinner.

GIUSEPPE VERDI CONDUCTING AN ORCHESTRA

From Prospero Bertani to Giuseppe Verdi, 1872

Reggio (Emilia), 7 May 1872

On the second of this month, attracted by the sensation your opera *Aida* was making, I went to Parma. Half an hour before the performance began I was already in my seat, no. 120. I admired the scenery, listened with great pleasure to the excellent singers, and took pains to let nothing escape me. After the performance was over, I asked myself whether I was satisfied. The answer was in the negative. I returned to Reggio and, on the way back in the railroad carriage, I listened to the verdicts of my fellow travellers. Nearly all of them agreed that *Aida* was a work of the highest rank.

Thereupon I conceived a desire to hear it again, and so on the fourth I returned to Parma. I made the most desperate efforts to obtain a reserved seat, and there was such a crowd that I had to spend 5 lire to see the performance in comfort.

I came to the following conclusion: the opera contains absolutely nothing thrilling or electrifying and, if it were not for the magnificent scenery, the audience would not sit through it to the end. It will fill the theatre a few more times and then gather dust in the archives. Now, my dear Signor Verdi, you can imagine my regret at having spent 32 lire for these two performances, and you will understand that this money preys on my mind like a terrible spectre. Therefore I address myself frankly and openly to you so that you may send me this sum. Here is the account:

Railroad: one way	2.60 lire
Railroad: return trip	3.30 ”
Theatre	8.00 ”
Disgustingly bad dinner at the station	2.0 ”
Multiplied by 2	= 15.90 lire x2
	= 31.80 lire

In the hope that you will extricate me from this dilemma, I am yours sincerely,

Bertani

My address: Bertani, Prospero; Via St. Domenico, No. 5

From Giuseppe Verdi to Giulio Ricordi

Dear Giulio,

Yesterday I received from Reggio [Emilia] a letter which is so amusing that I am sending it to you, asking you to carry out the commission I am about to give you . . .

Imagine if, to protect a child of a family <u>from the horrible spectres that disturb his peace</u>, I should not be disposed to pay that little bill he has brought to my attention! Therefore by means of your representative or a bank, please reimburse 27.80 lire in my name to this Signor Prospero Bertani, 5 Via St. Domenico. This isn't the entire sum for which he asks me, but . . . to pay for his dinner too! . . . No. He could very well have eaten at home!!!!! Of course he will send you a receipt for that sum and a note, by which he promises never again to go to hear my new operas, to avoid for himself the dangers of other spectres and for me the farce of paying him for another trip . . .

From Giulio Ricordi to Giuseppe Verdi

Milan, 16th May 1872

As soon as I received your last letter I wrote our correspondent in Reggio, who found the famous Signor Bertani, paid the money, and got the proper receipt!!! I am copying the letter and the receipt for the newspaper, and I shall return everything to you tomorrow. Oh, what fools there are in this world! But this is the best one yet!

The correspondent in Reggio writes me: 'I sent immediately for Bertani, who came to me right away. Advised of the reason for my invitation, he first showed surprise, but then he said: "<u>If Maestro Verdi reimburses me, this means that he has found what I wrote him to be correct. It's my duty to thank him, however, and I ask you do it for me.</u>"'

This one is even better!

Pleased to have discovered this rarity of the species, I send the most cordial greetings to you and Signora Peppina.

From Prospero Bertani to Giuseppe Verdi

15th May 1872

I, the undersigned, certify herewith that I have received the sum of 27.80 lire from Maestro Giuseppe Verdi, as reimbursement of my expenses for a trip to Parma to hear the opera *Aida*. The Maestro felt it was fair that this sum should be restored to me, since I did not find his opera to my taste. At the same time, it is agreed that I shall undertake no trip to hear any of the Maestro's new operas in the future, unless he takes all the expenses upon himself, whatever my opinion of his works may be.

In confirmation whereof I have affixed my signature,

Bertani, Prospero

'I NEVER WAS SO RELIEVED, SO FAR AS I CAN REMEMBER, IN MY LIFE, BY THE STOPPING OF ANY SOUND'

JOHN RUSKIN'S SCATHING REVIEW OF WAGNER'S OPERA
DIE MEISTERSINGER VON NÜRNBERG

Sometimes a friend may drag you to a concert that just isn't to your musical taste. Other times, you may dislike the performance so much that you have to invent new words in order to properly insult it. This at least was the experience of the critic John Ruskin, who found Richard Wagner's opera *Die Meistersinger von Nürnberg* to be the most 'tuneless, scrannelpipiest', 'blundering, boggling, baboon-blooded stuff' he had ever seen on stage.

Wagner was an established composer and theatre director who was known for writing both the music and the libretto for his operas. Wagner was a proponent of various new concepts in opera, such as the 'music drama', which aimed at nothing less than a complete synthesis of the arts in every performance. He also valued the orchestra as highly as his singers, considering the performance of both as integral to the success of a piece. His most famous works include *Der Ring des Nibelungen*, or 'Ring Cycle', of four dramatic operas based on Norse and Germanic mythology, *Tristan und Isolde*, and *Die Walküre*. Moreover, several of the pieces he composed for these operas are famous in their own right, including 'The Ride of the Valkyries', which has been used in iconic pop-culture media like *Star Wars* and *Apocalypse Now!*, and 'Bridal Chorus', instantly recognizable as the music most often played for brides walking down the aisle at their weddings.

Die Meistersinger von Nürnberg was Wagner's only comedic opera, and runs to a staggering four-and-a-half hours, not including the breaks between acts. For those who enjoyed it, the opera telling the story of love and music in sixteenth-century Nuremberg was a masterpiece; for those who did not, however, *Die Meistersinger* was a three-act test of endurance.

When the opera premiered in London in 1882, the polymath and art critic John Ruskin (1819–1900) unfortunately found himself in this latter camp. Ruskin bore a longstanding dislike for the German classical style, and yet was among the first to see Wagner's opera at Drury Lane Theatre. Having stewed in his seat through all four-and-a-half hours of *Die Meistersinger*, Ruskin utilized the full breadth of his literary arsenal to describe his hatred of the opera in this letter to the artist Georgiana Burne-Jones. Despite Ruskin's scathing review, *Die Meistersinger* remains one of the most popular of Wagner's operas, and all four-and-a-half 'beginningless, endless, topless, bottomless' hours of it are frequently staged around the world.

From John Ruskin to Georgiana Burne-Jones, 1882

30th June, 1882

. . . Of all the *bête*, clumsy, blundering, boggling, baboon-blooded stuff I ever saw on a human stage, that thing last night beat – so far as the acting and story went – and all of the affected, sapless, soulless, beginningless, endless, topless, bottomless, topsiturviest [*sic*], tuneless, scrannelpipiest [*sic*], tongs and boniest doggrel [*sic*] of sounds I ever endured the deadliness of, that eternity of nothing was the deadliest, so far as the sound went. I never was so relieved, so far as I can remember, in my life, by the stopping of any sound – not excepting railway whistles – as I was by the cessation of the cobbler's bellowing; even the serenader's caricatured twangle was a rest after it. As for the great '*Lied*', I never made out where it began or where it ended – except by the fellow's coming off the horse block. – Ever your lovingest [*sic*]

ST. C.

'THE ENTIRE THEATRE SHAKES WITH APPLAUSE. I AM SURE THAT IT LASTED FOR FIVE ENTIRE MINUTES'

ENRICO CARUSO REVELS IN THE SUCCESS OF HIS DEBUT
As Enrico Caruso prepared himself to take the stage at the Teatro Lirico opera house in Milan in 1897, he felt he was taking a leap of faith. Caruso (1873–1921) had arrived in the city just a month earlier as an ambitious young tenor eager to make his name in the capital of Italian opera. Though at first he struggled to attract attention, he was eventually offered the role of Araquil in the opera *La Navarraise*. While Caruso leaped at the opportunity, he was faced with the daunting task of mastering the role in only a few days. His trepidation was only compounded after several nerve-stricken rehearsals during which Caruso could barely shake the tremor from his voice. Consequently, as the singer lingered behind the curtain on the night of his debut, his anxieties must have weighed heavily on his mind.

In the end Caruso had nothing to fear: the performance was a wonderous success, and his stage fright dissipated when he was met by a thunderous applause from an enchanted audience. Caruso's relief at this success is palpable in this letter he wrote to his then lover and fellow opera singer, Ada Giachetti.

By 1902, Caruso had built on this initial success to establish himself as one of opera's rising stars. He had performed leading roles in opera houses across the length and breadth of Italy, including the famous La Scala in Milan, while on the international scene he had wowed audiences across South America, Egypt and Russia. No longer a fledgling prospect, Caruso was now moving within Italy's musical elite, commanding the respect of peers like Puccini, Giordano, Tetrazzini, Chaliapin and Toscanini.

By the time of his death in 1921, Caruso had sung in the finest and most prestigious venues all over the world, including a mammoth 800 performances at the Metropolitan Opera in New York City. What is more, he succeeded in breaking new ground by capitalizing on the emergence of the gramophone, and his recordings became some of the very first international 'hits'. Undoubtedly, Enrico Caruso had confirmed himself to be one of the first true music superstars.

ENRICO CARUSO DRESSED AS 'CANIO' FOR THE OPERA *PAGLIACCI*, 1908

From Enrico Caruso to Ada Giachetti, 1897

4th November 1897

Victory! Victory! In the true sense of the word. Victory over everyone, and even without consciously planning it, because I was completely absorbed by my role. Just imagine, if I had performed like I did during the dress rehearsals, they would have officially discharged me! But no, it was not like that, quite the opposite. Why? Because my adored *Mimma* [Ada] was praying for me, isn't it true? Yes . . . I sensed it, as I was feeling very proud of myself. I have to admit that I was quite nervous beforehand, because my voice was a little heavy, especially on the low notes, but when my moment came, after doing the sign of the cross, and thinking of all of my loved ones, off I went. I sang my first duet, and it was splendid, especially its *tempo*, and especially if we compare it to the day before, when it had been a complete disaster, me being petrified. So, I finished the duet with a round of applause, which was only contained by the start of the following segment. Then, I am immediately on stage again, to sing my little romance [*romanza*] and, at the end of this piece, which ends with a wonderful B flat, the entire theatre shakes with applause. I am sure that it lasted for five entire minutes, as I stood there motionless on stage, celebrated by applause, again and again, my public shouting *encore*! So I granted them this pleasure and had to sing it again, and it was better than the first time, and I was rewarded by renewed appreciation.

My darling, if only you could have been with me! I was thinking of you during that very moment, while my audience was applauding me. Oh! If my Ada were here, how proud would she be of me? [. . .]

So, after my *encore*, I finished with a little duet together with another tenor, and off I went. I then came back on stage once again for the *finale*. I was supposed to be wounded and I had to sing another duet with my lady, then it all had to end with my death on stage. What joy, if only it could have been you, instead of that woman! My fall would have been magnificent, but in that moment I was not thinking of you, and our public called us out seven times, after the end of the show, with unanimous applause.

I do not want to tire you now with my lengthy descriptions, you will be able to read all this in the newspapers I shall send you.

So, my future is now assured, but this means really nothing to me, without its core happiness: you. So if my career goes hand in hand with my happiness, then all will be well, otherwise I do not know what to do with all these glories and these achievements!

My love! I am so joyful now that I know that I can see this wonderful path ahead of me, but I am worried about having to walk on it all by myself. This is just intolerable, and I simply would not know how to do this by myself. I would certainly lose myself, and end up on a perilous path. What can I do to find the direct path? I need my little adorable *Adina*, who, alone, is able to lead me on the right path towards the right destination.

Milano 4/11/97

Mia Ada!

Vittoria! Vittoria! Nel vero senso della parola. Vittoria riportata su tutti e senza che neanche io ne avessi potuto pensare, perché incerto della parte in tutto e per tutto. Figurati che credevo, di cantare come alla prova generale che mi davano un bel comodo in carta bollata. Invece non è stato così, perché! Perché la mia adorata mamma pregavi per me. Non è vero che pregavi per me? Sì — io lo sentivo, perché ero franco di me stesso. Avevo un po' di dubbio prima di uscire perché avevo la voce specialmente nei casi pesante molto; ma poi venuto il momento d'uscire, dopo d'essermi segnato, e passato nel mio pensiero tutti i miei più cari, sono uscito. Ho cantato il mio primo duetto stupendamente specialmente per il tempo, perché la sera prima non ne indovinavo nes...

FROM THE JAMES DRAKE COLLECTION

'I AM <u>INEXPRESSIBLY</u> HAPPY: AND FEEL AS IF OIL HAD BEEN POURED INTO THE GROANING MACHINERY OF THE UNIVERSE'

MAURICE BARING CELEBRATES DAME ETHEL SMYTH'S SUCCESS

As a queer feminist who enjoyed nothing more than hunting and smoking, Ethel Smyth did not quite fit the mould for the archetypal Edwardian woman. She was not demure but gregarious; not timid but forthright. She was, put simply, a woman of conviction, committed to pursuing her every ambition. One such ambition was to become a world-leading composer. It was an aspiration Smyth (1858–1944) had held from the age of 12, and one she achieved to the fullest.

Smyth's composition style is defined by a bold, sophisticated late-Romantic aesthetic heavily influenced by the likes of Brahms and Wagner. This rich sound was best captured in her operatic compositions, most notably *Der Wald* (*The Forest*, 1902) and *Les naufrageurs* (*The Wreckers*, 1906), which are marked for their rich orchestral combinations and innovative use of harmonic language.

Despite exhibiting great skill as an operatic composer, however, over the course of her career Smyth faced a continual struggle for recognition. Composing, and in particular opera, have until recently been an almost exclusively male domain, and many theatre managers were reluctant to play host to a female composer. For her first opera, *Fantasio*, Smyth was advised to publish the piece under a male pseudonym if she wanted any chance of it being performed. Even when she did manage to have her work performed, critics spent most of their time determining whether her music expressed a masculine or feminine temperament. Such obstacles failed to dull Smyth's efforts to have her music performed, however, and in 1902 she achieved a breakthrough when she had *Der Wald* performed at Covent Garden.

News of the success soon spread among Smyth's many friends, and several wrote to her with congratulations. By far the most heartfelt of these letters was that sent by 'man of letters' Maurice Baring. Though he was unable to attend the performance in person, it was enough for him to know that his dear friend was finally receiving the recognition she deserved.

The following years held many further accolades for Smyth. In 1903, she would become the first woman to have an opera performed at the Metropolitan Opera in New York. Back home, her brilliance caught the attention of Queen Victoria, who bestowed on Smyth a damehood for her services to music. As if these achievements were not enough to cement her name in history, Smyth also became heavily involved in the woman's suffrage movement, and she composed a piece entitled *March of the Women* which quickly became the battle cry of the movement.

Smyth's name and her contribution to music faded into relative obscurity in the years that followed her passing, a fate indicative of the resistance she faced during her lifetime. In recent years, however, her cultural contribution has begun to be rediscovered, with recognition given to the great strides she made for British female composers.

DAME ETHEL SMYTH, C. 1901

From Maurice Baring to Dame Ethel Smyth, 1902

ROME.

July 19, 1902.

9 a.m.

Beloved E.,

I got a telegram from Grahame early this morning and telegraphed to you immediately. I am *inexpressibly* happy: and feel as if oil had been poured into the groaning machinery of the universe (just as one sometimes feels as if the devil had thrown a handful of pebbles into it).

You know that my faith in the *Wald* has been constant, unshaken and unshakable from the first day you played me '*Heil'ger Wald*' on your piano at One Oak, and I knew – as Galileo knew some fact about the sun – that sooner or later it would force recognition: but it's satisfactory that it should be now, and not when we are dead; and doubly satisfactory after Berlin and *all the obstacles*. In fact, I think you have accomplished something as difficult as Hannibal crossing the Alps; I am so happy; longing to see the newspapers. I asked Grahame to *abonner* me at a Press Agency. I hope he will. It was sad that I wasn't there, *for me*. Last night I sat, watch in hand, during dinner and when it was 9.15 here, 8.15, I suppose, in London, I thought of the *Wald* beginning and nearly sobbed.

The moral is one should always live in London, because if one doesn't one misses everything. I haven't dared mention leave yet: it depends on a number of things: I may get leave in August – I may not. I won't bore you with any more at this moment. This is only to remind you of what you know already, *i.e.* my utter *joy* at your success. I should like to have seen Aunt M'aimée's face. I hope someone will write me details.

Yours affec., M.

'EXCUSE THIS OUTBURST . . . BUT THE WHOLE CONCATENATION OF ROTTEN, DESTRUCTIVE THINGS HAS MADE ME VERY ANGRY AND DISAPPOINTED'

LEONARD BERNSTEIN BEMOANS THE POOR STATE OF THE ARTS

When Leonard Bernstein, the renowned conductor and composer of such timeless pieces as the Broadway musical *West Side Story* (1957) and the theatrical piece *Mass* (1971), was a student at Harvard University, he had a unique party trick. With just a piano and Aaron Copland's *Piano Variations* (1930), he could clear the room at any social gathering in less than three minutes. For most, the severe and dissonant style of Copland's piece was an acquired taste. For Bernstein (1918–90), however, it was one of the finest works ever composed by the man who, in his mind, was going to reinvigorate American music.

Having never met Copland, Bernstein could only imagine such a musician as a towering old sage set aloof from common society through his mastery of the art of composition. As would become all too clear on meeting the composer in 1937, however, Bernstein realised his estimations were a little off the mark.

Their meeting took place entirely by chance when Bernstein – then a 19-year-old freshman student – travelled to New York to see a modern dance concert. He was to meet with some friends at the box-office and, on arriving, found they had brought in tow a man he later described as small, spectacled and with a wide friendly grin. The stranger was in fact Bernstein's musical idol and, to his amazement, he was seated right next to him.

Following the performance, Bernstein and his companions were invited back to Copland's New York apartment to join in on the composer's 37th birthday celebrations. Once there Bernstein immediately gravitated towards the piano, where he boldly began to play Copland's *Piano Variations* before its maker. Rather than clearing the room, on this occasion Bernstein's confident rendition made him the heart of the party, and his performance sparked an enduring friendship between the two musicians.

For Bernstein, Copland became a teacher, a confidant and surrogate father-figure with whom he would share a 50-year long correspondence in which they discussed everything from the art of composition to the national identity of American music. The letter included here was sent just four months after their memorable first meeting. In it Bernstein vented his frustrations to his new-found mentor as he decried the state of the arts. Against the backdrop of increasing tensions in Europe, he took the poor state of the arts to be symbolic of the deterioration of civil society. His only relief was in knowing there were still sound-minded composers like Copland to counteract these worrying trends.

LEONARD BERNSTEIN CONDUCTING *SONGFEST*

From Leonard Bernstein to Aaron Copland, 1938

22nd March 1938

God damn it, Aaron,

Why practise Chopin Mazurkas? Why practise even the Copland *Variations?* The week has made me so sick, Aaron, that I can't breathe any more. The whole superfluousness of art shows up at a time like this, and the whole futility of spending your life in it. I take it seriously – seriously enough to want to be with it constantly till the day I die. But why? With millions of people going mad – madder every day because of a most mad man strutting across borders – with every element that we thought had refined human living and made what we called civilization being actively forgotten deliberately thrown back like rail-road tracks when you look hard enough at them – what chance is there? Art is more than ever now proved entertainment – people, we thought, were ready, after two thousand years of refining Christianity, to look for entertainment as such; to look for things that come out of the category of vital necessity! And so we were willing to spend our lives creating that entertainment. Aaron, it's not feasible; it's a damned dirty disappointment.

Then came the climax of the week. Cara Version – whoever she is; to me she looks like an enlarged porcupine – had advertised for weeks that she was going to give in the Jordan Hall here, a whole program of modern music. I was all excited; it was unprecedented, and very courageous of her in this dead city, etc., etc. And I put so much hope in that damned concert. It came: and I find it difficult to talk about it. It was a tremendous program – Malipiero, Kodály, Hindemith – and – joy of joys! – the Copland *Variations*. That, I guess, was the premiere in Boston. Well, to get to the point, I don't know whether you knew it was going to be played here, but if you did, how did you allow it?

In short, she gave really no performance at all. I can stand a bad performance, but not *no* performance. She began the thing wrong, played about two measures, skipped some variations, got lost again, skipped about 5 pages, played a few measures out of temp – entirely without any discernment, without any idea of rhythm – and kept this up (playing little measures from choice variations) until she reached the coda. Then she played about half of it and called it a day. I was purple – I wish I could let you know how incredibly bad it was. It was the work of an imbecile. I left then and broke dishes in the Georgian cafeteria.

Do you see what that farce meant, Aaron? The few people that were there thought she was wonderful – such a *touch*! (!!!) They tried to look intellectually intelligent about the music when the whole performance was one of bafflement! The one little chance that this little town gets to hear some modern piano stuff – (nobody dares to do it as a recital) – we find instead the complete distortion of the whole art, a perversion of these people's attitude when we need every resource to show them the right thing, correctly done. And where did this foul woman get press notices for her folder? Aaron, find that woman and have her put away. She's fatal.

Excuse this outburst, Aaron, but the whole concatenation of rotten, destructive things has made me very angry and disappointed. At Harvard the situation is aggravated by these horrible musical dolls who infest the place. I find it almost impossible to stand. Thank God for you. Our last hope is in the work you are doing.

Leonard Bernstein

'MY DEAR MASTER, I ASSURE YOU THAT SO FAR AS I AM CONCERNED YOU ARE INTENSELY WRONG'

EVERY MAN HIS OWN MUSIC CRITIC? ARNOLD SCHOENBERG DEBATES THE ETIQUETTE OF MUSICAL CRITICISM

The Oxford Companion to Music defines music criticism as 'the intellectual activity of formulating judgements on the value and degree of excellence of individual works of music, or whole groups or genres'. It is an apt definition, yet begs the question of *who* can determine a musician's 'value' or 'excellence'. In other words, *who* is allowed to legitimately label themselves a critic of music?

For some musicians the legitimacy of music criticism as a discipline should be questioned in and of itself (Richard Strauss once suggested the profession should be 'abolished'). Such criticisms are targeted towards those individuals employed by newspapers and magazines to produce insightful literary judgements of performances taking place across the towns and cities of Europe and the wider world. That Strauss should wish the demise of this practice is reflective of the contentious relationship the musician and critic have held for over three centuries.

Between the eighteenth and twentieth centuries, when the print media were at their height, a critic's opinion could make or break a musician. Before video and social media, those who could not attend a performance were reliant on the opinions of the critic; they were, as Aaron Copland once put it, the 'middle man between the public and the creative artist'. Though he also reportedly described them as a 'menace', Copland could not deny that amicable relations between the musician and critic were an 'absolute necessity'. Others were less forgiving.

One only need look at the very public falling out between Arnold Schoenberg and the renowned music critic Olin Downes (1886–1955) that played out in the *New York Times*, for instance, to see his views as more akin to those of Strauss. The spat started following Downes' disparaging review of Gustav Mahler's Seventh Symphony. Taking umbrage at his close friend's music being subjected to such scorn, Schoenberg wrote to Downes questioning the credentials.

On receiving the letter, Downes decided to publish it, along with his response, in the following edition of *The Times*, believing it would be of interest to its readers. In it he defended his right to judge, arguing that the members of the musical world must expect to be subject to critique outside their circles of peer review.

Schoenberg refused to back down, reiterating his point that criticism from those with no musical credentials beyond an inflated opinion of their artistic taste was inherently unfounded.

From Olin Downes to Arnold Schoenberg, 1948

December 3, 1948

Dear Mr Schoenberg:

I have read with interest and appreciation your letter concerning my review of Mitropoulos' recent performance of Mahler's Seventh Symphony. You say some interesting things which it is a pleasure to read. I must add, however, in frankness, that some of your remarks appear to me to be illogical.

I entirely disagree with you that your sentiment about '*Chacun à son goût*' ['Each to their own tastes'] is 'a great mistake'. It simply means that in reviewing a work I express my convinced opinion, but that everyone else who listens is entirely <u>entitled to his</u> own opinions and his own tastes in the matter. It also means that while I am frank to say as I did say and as I completely believe that this symphony of Mahler's is detestably bad music, that others who think as you do, for example, have an equal right to their conclusions. I think this is the very essence of <u>fair critical</u> practice. I do not consider myself a high priest of art, I do not pretend that my values of any music are conclusive. I do not even claim that I can tell at a single glance at a score whether the music is good or bad, whether it will perish quickly or last onward into infinity.

I must ask you a question. Do you really mean seriously to claim to me that composers, even the greatest composers, are as a rule fair or unbiased critics of other composers' works? Frankly, I can hardly credit you with such an unhistoric statement. Do you think, for example, that a composer who states that Beethoven's Seventh Symphony makes him ripe for the madhouse, is in the least intelligent or fair in this, his written judgement? The name of the 'critic' was Carl Maria von Weber. Do you take seriously what Schumann wrote about Wagner's *Tannhäuser*, or what Berlioz said on the same subject, or what Debussy said of Beethoven, that he was a bore? These instances could be multiplied indefinitely. I am afraid that the greatest names in the history of musical composition do not connote either balance or perspective of musical judgement. For a final illustration of this obvious fact, let me quote you what an editorial board of five of the greatest composers in Russia said when they were asked by Koussevitzky, as a publisher, whether he should publish Stravinsky's *Petroushka*. The score was unanimously rejected by these high and mighty gentlemen as being 'not music'!

And then, Mr. Schoenberg, you really hurt my feelings. Apparently you think that I do not read scores. I hope you don't infer also that I am incapable of this. I can even tell you that the score of Mahler's Seventh Symphony has been in my library for years, while as for piano arrangements of his music, I have gone through half of his Fifth Symphony on two pianos and gotten up from the instrument being really unable to stomach any farther such vulgar music. I don't even find the thematic examples that you quote from the Mahler Symphony, either particularly distinguished as melodies, or even as representing the best thematic elements of that unfortunate work.

Now as to inconsistencies. My dear master, I assure you that so far as I am concerned you are intensely wrong. Why do you assume that I have written 'in an unfriendly manner about Mahler and am now afraid to depart from a primary judgement'. Why? In the first place you are uninformed on the subject. I have found things to praise and to enjoy, for example, in Mahler's *Lied von der Erde*, which I formerly liked a good deal more than I do now, because its self-pity and sentimentalism is rather unpleasant to me. I enjoy pages of his first Symphony. I have gone 'completely overboard' upon the first half of his Eighth, etc., etc. You seem to think that because I wrote well of your Five Pieces this season that I have done so because I wrote well of them years ago. I can tell you frankly that I do not try to remember what I have writen [sic] in the past about music that I listen to in the present. But I think I do remember that I cursed your 'Five Pieces' to high heaven and expected that I would dislike them the other night. To my surprise, I found that I liked them and realized on hearing them this time how much effect their principles had upon modern music.

I am afraid I must unhappily come to the conclusion that I think very badly of the Mahler Symphony and that you think very well of it and that this is merely another case of critics, and their readers, disagreeing; as, thank God, they will always disagree, and in the expression of their convictions greatly contribute to the development of an art.

With best wishes, I am

Sincerely yours, Olin Downes

From Arnold Schoenberg to Olin Downes

December 21, 1948

Dear Mr. Downes:

Before responding to some of the points of your very interesting letter, I must mention that I did not expect that in its imperfect form of a private letter it would be published. I was in a fighting mood caused by your criticism of Mahler. I felt this can be a fight for death and life, in which case one is not obliged to worry about the fairness and correctness of the blows one deals out. If they only hurt.

Nevertheless I should not have pretended that you do not study scores and that you are prejudiced by your own previous judgements. This, however, can not have hurt you as much, as I am hurt by your reproach of illogicality – there is nothing worse to me than that. Fortunately you can not prove Mahler's vulgarity and neither can I prove my attack on your musicianship. It seems to me that the scale goes down on your side and that a true equilibrium requires some additional weight in favor of my logic.

In your letter to Mr. Mitropoulos . . . you say that music is to you like a religion and you reserve for yourself the right to be intolerant against a believer of a different faith. I would call this the claim of a fighter. But I will rather tell you a story:

Several years ago an announcer over a nationwide network broadcast attacks on my music to a crowd of two and a half million listeners. I thought this man is an . . . Oh perhaps it is better even now not to tell you what I thought. But at this time I was belligerently desiring to tell all the audience what I was thinking.

You write? '*Chacun à son goût*,' and you are fortunate enough to tell hundred thousands [*sic*] of your readers, which is your taste. But how can I inform those two and a half million radio listeners that their announcer is . . . wrong. One who possesses such an unlimited power must have a sense of responsibility.

You claim the right of a fighter, the right to be intolerant. Is it logical to deny the opponent the same rights if he is infuriated to a degree which makes him refusing to see the forest as long as he has to conquer individual trees.

It is the word 'taste' which excites me.

In my vocabulary it stands for 'arrogance and superiority complex of the mediocrity'

And:

Taste is sterile – it can not reproduce.

And:

Taste is applicable only to the lower zones of human feelings, to the material ones. It is no yardstick in spiritual matters.

And:

Taste functions mainly as a restricting factor, as a negation to every problem, as a minus to every number.

'*Chacun à son goût*' wants to make believe that there exists an enormous number of ways to be extremely personal – but there is not enough caviar, or gold or good luck in the world for everybody. And those '*chacuns*' must share the little '*goût*' which exists, which of course is a commonplace mass product, with very few marks of personal distinction.

You write that your preference to your taste means simply that you express your personal opinion and that everybody is entitled to his own. 'Entiteld' [*sic*] is the right word. Has he who disagrees with you a chance of telling this to the same audience as often as he disagrees?

Furthermore: you do notpretend [*sic*] 'that your ideas of music are conclusive.' Contrast this lightharted [*sic*] standpoint to the standpoint of an artist like Mahler, who would have preferred to die a thousand times, than to being [*sic*] forced to believe he was wrong.

I hope you will understand why your condemnation of a great man and composer on the basis of personal taste enraged me. Then I will gladly admit that another cause to this fury derived from the fact that between 1898 and 1908 I had spoken about Mahler in the same manner, as you do today. For that I made good subsequently by adoration.

And frankly, this is what I resent most: Why should you not also have expirienced [*sic*] such transformations in your mind, from Saulus to Paulus with many of the greats in the arts, including besides Brahms and Wagner, Strauss and Mahler, even Mozart and Beethoven?

Still, I am not a windbag of an unsolid fixation, who gamingly [*sic*] changes his position for no intelligible reason. All these changes corresponded to my progressive development in various phases of my life before maturity was reached. A very characteristic experience of mine may serve as an illustration: Between 1925 and 1935 I did not dare to read or listened [*sic*] to Mahler's music. I was afraid my aversion against it in a preceding period might return. Fortunately, when I heard in Los Angeles a moderately satisfactory performance of the Second, I was just enchanted as ever before: It had not lost [any] of its persuasiveness.

Now finally to your question whether I believe composers are as a rule fair or unbiased critics of other composers: I think they are in first line fighters for their own musical ideas. The ideas of other composers are their enemies. You can not restrict a fighter. His blows are correct when they hit hard, and only then is he fair. Thus I do not resent what Schumann said about Wagner, or Hugo Wolf about Brahms. But I resent what Hanslick said against Wagner, Wolf, Mahler and Strauss fought for life and death of there [*sic*] ideas.

But you fight only for principles, or rather the application of principles.

At the end I can tell you that I agree with the last of your points: ' . . . that this is merely another case of critics and their readers, disagreeing as, thank God, they will always disagree, and in the expression of their convictions greatly contribute to the development of an art.' – negatively or positively.

With best wishes, also for Christmas and New Year,

I am most sincerely yours

Arnold Schoenberg

CHAPTER SIX

THE ROAD TO SUCCESS

It takes ten years, suggests the received wisdom, to be an overnight success. The road travelled for those ten years is not, of course, paved solely with successes of incrementally greater magnitude until, finally, the great – overnight – success is achieved. Instead it is paved with mistakes, missteps, failures and humiliations. For every moment experienced by a 20-year-old Schumann ('there is an adorably clear golden sky . . . my cigar has an excellent flavour; and, in short, the world is very fair . . .') there are many, many more of the kind recorded by Leonard Cohen ('Walking through the city, insisting that no one follow, feeling either black or golden, dead to lust, tired of ambition, a lazy student of my own pain . . .'). It is how one reacts to the latter rather than the former that suggests the likelihood of eventual success.

Life on the road to success is tough. The letters in this chapter illustrate just how tough, and if we were to isolate just one theme from this wide-ranging, century-spanning collection it would surely be 'sacrifice'.

It is easier to sympathize with those who write of the sacrifices they make on the path to success than those who write of the sacrifices required *by* success. If the whining of the ultra-privileged and ultra-successful irritates you then you are in good company, though: Frank Sinatra, via *Calendar* magazine, gives George Michael – 'the reluctant popstar' – a metaphorical slap, encouraging him to 'loosen up. Swing, man. Dust off those gossamer wings and fly yourself to the moon of your choice and be grateful to carry the baggage we've all had to carry since those lean nights of sleeping on buses and helping the driver unload the instruments.' Wise enough words, but his outright dismissal of the 'tragedy of fame' rings somewhat hollow in the context of some of the other letters in this chapter.

Sinatra's definition of 'tragedy' is an insult to real tragedy. And his is a difficult letter to read in the knowledge – which we of course possess – that George Michael's life ended, for reasons related to the fast-living typical of the very famous, on Christmas Day 2016, at the age of 53. Whether this was a 'tragedy' as opposed to simply very sad it is left up to the reader to decide, but it is certainly closer to the tragic than Sinatra's 'empty joint that hasn't seen a paying customer since Saint Swithin's day [sic]'.

But the sacrifice of which we read is wide-ranging and often subtly articulated, particularly by the women featured in this chapter. Zitkála-Šá's letter to her former fiancé Carlos Montezuma concludes with a sad little paragraph in which we discern the flicker of a torch carried still: the light illuminating the small sacrifices – at the expense of her musical career – made at the behest of the man she did marry. And Janis Joplin's letter to her parents is a snapshot of what has clearly been an ongoing (and hardly unique) family discussion about the young Janis's career plans: 'I'm awfully sorry to be such a disappointment to you' seems suffused with genuine regret.

The observation cannot be avoided that the letters in this chapter, as well as dwelling on sacrifice (if not 'tragedy'), expose talented musicians and composers through the ages as temperamental, insecure, emotionally volatile sorts. They lash out: they complain bitterly about not very much at all; they swing wildly between utter lack of self-belief and iron-clad confidence; and they demand – like Gustav Mahler in his extraordinary letter to his wife Alma – appalling sacrifice from those whom they love on the altar of their own vanity. And, just occasionally, they see things in perspective.

It is perhaps Arthur Sullivan's youthful letter, in which he (admittedly with some accuracy) diagnoses the ailment afflicting music in England, and how he proposes to treat that ailment, that serves as a good jumping-off point for this chapter. Well buried it might be, but as you read of the sacrifices made by those travelling their own roads, actually or metaphorically, and as you read letters written in the heat of the moment, lashing out at others and self, listen for the sentiment with which Sullivan closes his letter. Without it, no matter how cynical a letter-writer might wish you to believe they are, success could never have been achieved: 'hope and persevere is my motto.'

'HOW COULD I POSSIBLY ADMIT AN INFIRMITY IN THE *ONE SENSE* WHICH SHOULD HAVE BEEN MORE PERFECT IN ME THAN IN OTHERS?'

THE CRUELLEST FATE FOR A MUSICIAN: BEETHOVEN'S STRUGGLE WITH HEARING LOSS

The early years of the 1800s marked a difficult period in Ludwig van Beethoven's life. While it was an incredibly productive and successful time in his career (in 1800 alone he composed more than five pieces and premiered his first symphony, with his 'Moonlight' Sonata and Second Symphony being debuted in 1801 and 1802 respectively), Beethoven (1770–1827) was also suffering with intense anxiety and depression on account of his increasing deafness.

He had first reported difficulties with his hearing in 1798, and by 1802 it had grown to be an intense cause of anguish for the young composer. On the advice of his doctor, Beethoven travelled to the idyllic village of Heiligenstadt (now a district of Vienna) to convalesce, in an attempt to ease his health anxieties; as this infamous letter testifies, however, Beethoven found little in the countryside to assuage his melancholy.

The impression Beethoven gives in this letter, now referred to as the Heiligenstadt Testament, to his brothers Carl and Johann, is that his hearing loss was both sudden and stark. In reality the decline was far more protracted, and he experienced fluctuations in his hearing for several years. Nonetheless, Beethoven's fear

at becoming completely deaf before even reaching his thirtieth
birthday is palpable, and the letter gives a harrowing insight into
the dark corners of his mind as he felt the future he had envisioned
for himself as a musician slipping away.

Fortunately, Beethoven never found reason to send the letter to
his brothers as he bravely clawed his way up from the depths of
his depression and returned to Vienna with a renewed vision of his
future. Furthermore, while his hearing loss continued to cause him
anguish, it by no means incapacitated his immense musical gift, and
the years following the Heiligenstadt Testament saw him compose
his grandest music yet.

BEETHOVEN WITH THE MANUSCRIPT OF THE *MISSA SOLEMNIS*, BY
JOSEPH KARL STIELER, 1820

From Ludwig van Beethoven to Carl and Johann Beethoven, 1802

6th October 1802

For my brothers Carl and [Johann] Beethoven.

O ye men who think or say that I am malevolent, stubborn or
misanthropic, how greatly do ye wrong me, you do not know the
secret causes of my seeming, from childhood my heart and mind were
disposed to the gentle feeling of good will, I was even ever eager to
accomplish great deeds, but reflect now that for 6 years I have been
in a hopeless case, aggravated by senseless physicians, cheated year
after year in the hope of improvement, finally compelled to face the
prospect of a *lasting malady* (whose cure will take years or, perhaps,
be impossible), born with an ardent and lively temperament, even
susceptible to the diversions of society, I was compelled early to
isolate myself, to live in loneliness, when I at times tried to forget
all this, O how harshly was I repulsed by the doubly sad experience
of my bad hearing, and yet it was impossible for me to say to men
speak louder, shout, for I am deaf, Ah how could I possibly admit an
infirmity in the *one sense* which should have been more perfect in me
than in others, a sense which I once possessed in highest perfection,
a perfection such as few surely in my profession enjoy or ever have
enjoyed – O I cannot do it, therefore forgive me when you see me
draw back when I would gladly mingle with you, my misfortune
is doubly painful because it must lead to my being misunderstood,
for me there can be no recreation in society of my fellows, refined
intercourse, mutual exchange of thought, only just as little as the
greatest needs command may I mix with society, I must live like an
exile, if I approach near to people a hot terror seizes upon me, a
fear that I may be subjected to the danger of letting my condition be
observed – thus it has been during the last half year which I spent
in the country, commanded by my intelligent physician to spare my
hearing as much as possible, in this almost meeting my present natural
disposition, although I sometimes ran counter to it yielding to my
inclination for society, but what a humiliation when one stood beside

me and heard a flute in the distance and *I heard nothing* or someone heard the *shepherd singing* and again I heard nothing, such incidents brought me to the verge of despair, but little more and I would have put an end to my life – only art it was that withheld me, ah it seemed impossible to leave the world until I had produced all that I felt called upon to produce, and so I endured this wretched existence – truly wretched, an excitable body which a sudden change can throw from the best into the worst state – Patience – it is said I must now choose for my guide, I have done so, I hope my determination will remain firm to endure until it pleases the inexorable parcæ [*sic*] to break the thread, perhaps I shall get better, perhaps not, I am prepared. Forced already in my 28th year to become a philosopher, O it is not easy, less easy for the artist than for any one else – Divine One thou lookest [*sic*] into my inmost soul, thou knowest it, thou knowest that love of man and desire to do good live therein. O men, when some day you read these words, reflect that ye did me wrong and let the unfortunate one comfort himself and find one of his kind who despite all the obstacles of nature yet did all that was in his power to be accepted among worthy artists and men. You my brothers Carl and [Johann] as soon as I am dead if Dr Schmid is still alive ask him in my name to describe my malady and attach this document to the history of my illness so that so far as is possible at least the world may become reconciled with me after my death. At the same time I divide it fairly, bear with and help each other, what injury you have done me you know was long ago forgiven. To you brother Carl I give special thanks for the attachment you have displayed towards me of late. It is my wish that your lives may be better and freer from care than I have had, recommend *virtue* to your children, it alone can give happiness, not money, I speak from experience, it was virtue that upheld me in misery, to it next to my art I owe that fact that I did not end my life by suicide – Farewell and love each other – I thank all my friends, particularly *Prince Lichnowsky and Professor Schmid* – I desire that the instruments from Prince L. be preserved by one of you but let no quarrel result from this, so soon as they can serve you a better purpose sell them, how glad will I be if I can still be helpful to you in my grave – with joy I hasten towards death — if it comes before I shall have had an opportunity to show all my artistic capacities it will still come too early for me despite my hard fate and I shall probably wish that it had come later — but even then I am satisfied, will it not free me from a state of endless suffering? Come when thou wilt I shall meet thee bravely — Farewell and do not wholly forget me when I am dead, I deserve this of you in having often in life thought of you how to make you happy be so —

Ludwig van Beethoven

Heiligenstadt October 6 1802

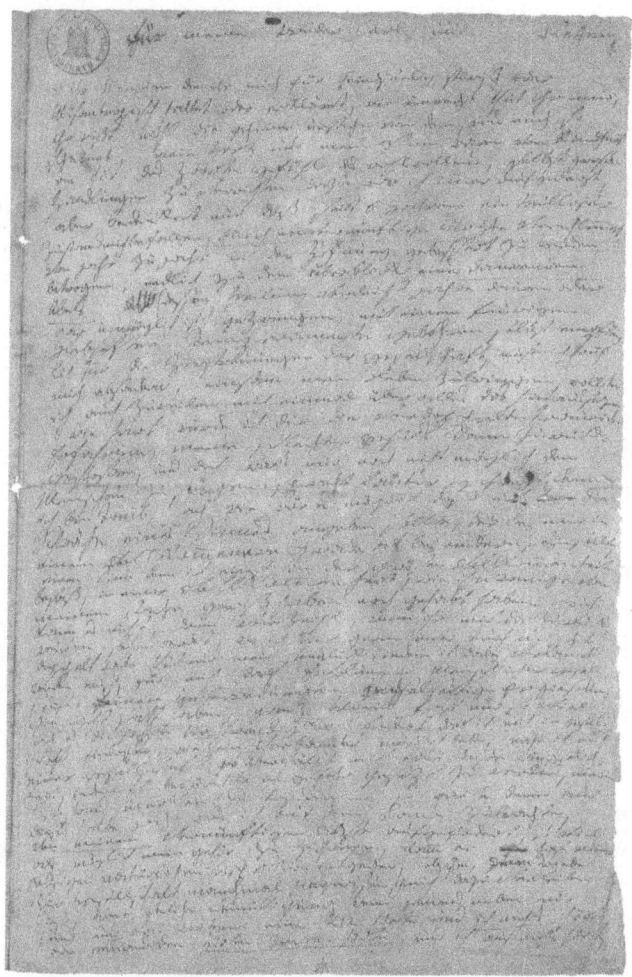

'BEETHOVEN'S HEILIGENSTAEDTER TESTAMENT, WIKIMEDIA COMMONS'

'MY LIFE HAS BEEN FOR TWENTY YEARS ONE LONG
STRUGGLE BETWEEN POETRY AND PROSE, OR, LET US
SAY, MUSIC AND LAW'

ROBERT SCHUMANN WEIGHS UP HIS FUTURE AS A MUSICIAN

There comes a point in every budding musician's life when they
must decide their future. It is an age-old dilemma, and one which
all artists must face: do they appease their family and get a safe,
'normal' job, or do they pursue their dreams, take the risk and try
to forge a career as an artist? In 1830, such a question weighed
heavily on the mind of Robert Schumann.

Schumann (1810–56) was born into a prosperous family living
in the city of Zwickau, Saxony. The family had no direct musical
connections, though Schumann's father, August, a bookseller and
publisher by trade, was eager for his children to explore their artistic
interests. Of his sons, Robert demonstrated a particular aptitude
for music, and August decided to buy him a Viennese Streicher
grand piano to support his development. Efforts were also made
to arrange lessons with the Royal Orchestra conductor in Dresden,
Carl Maria von Weber, however the death of both him and August
Schumann in 1826 foiled the plan.

The death of his father presented a crucial crossroad in
Schumann's future. A stipulation in August's will required that
Robert complete two years of university studies in order to receive
his inheritance; though reluctant, Schumann eventually conceded
to familial pressure and enrolled at the University of Heidelberg to
study law. He quickly developed a reputation as an absent-minded
student, however, and substituted late-night library sessions for
piano lessons. He kept this pattern for almost three years up until
his twentieth birthday in 1830, when he finally 'came of age' and
could legally take control of his own future.

While other 20-year-olds may be sleeping off a headache or
perhaps even still partying at dawn the day after their birthday,

Schumann put pen to paper to write a confessional letter to his mother that would finally end his grand charade and reveal the true nature of his studies in Heidelberg.

Though his dreams were grand and well intentioned, Robert Schumann unfortunately never quite managed to realize them. An injury that effectively paralysed his right index finger hampered any hopes of becoming a concert pianist, and much to his dismay his compositions struggled to achieve popularity during his lifetime.

ROBERT SCHUMANN

From Robert Schumann to Johanna Schumann, 1830

Heidelberg, 30 July 1830

Good Morning, Mamma!

How shall I describe to you my bliss at this moment! The spirit-lamp is flaming and spluttering under the coffee-pot; there is an adorably clear golden sky, and the spirit of the morning is abroad in all its freshness. Then your letter lies before me, revealing a perfect mine of affection, sagacity and virtue; my cigar has an excellent flavour; and, in short, the world is very fair at times – at least, to early risers.

My life here does not lack sunshine and blue sky, but I miss my cicerone, Rosen. The von H.'s, two brothers from Pomerania, whom I knew well, left for Italy a week ago; so I am left much to my own devices – that is, I am very happy or very miserable, as the fit takes me. Then, too, I sometimes work myself into a fever as I think over my past. My life has been for twenty years one long struggle between poetry and prose, or, let us say, music and law. My aims were as high in practical life as in art. I hoped to find scope for my energies and my powers of overcoming difficulties in a wide sphere of work. But what prospects are there, particularly Saxony, for an ordinary plebian, who has neither interest nor fortune, nor any real love for pettifogging legal details? At Leipzig I never troubled myself about my career, but dreamed and pottered away my time without any tangible results; here I have worked better, but my stay in both places has only tended to strengthen my leaning towards art. Now I stand at the crossroads, trembling before the question, Whither? My own instinct points to art, and I believe it to be the right road, but it has always seemed to me – you will not be hurt if I whisper it lovingly – that you rather barred my way in that direction. I quite see your excellent motherly reasons, known to both of

us as 'a precarious future' and 'an uncertain livelihood'. But let
us look a little further. A man can know no greater torment
than to look forward to an unhappy, empty and lifeless future
of his own planning; but neither is it easy for him to choose a
profession directly opposed to that for which he was destined
from his youth. Such a change means patience, confidence and
a rapid training. My fancy is young, and sheds its halo over the
artist-life; I have also arrived at the certainty that, given a good
teacher and six years' steady, hard work, I shall be able to hold
my own against any pianist, for pianoforte-playing is merely a
matter of mechanical perfection. I have, besides, an occasional
flight of fancy, and what is perhaps a real inspiration to compose.
This brings me to the question – which shall I choose? I can only
make my mark in one or the other. I tell myself that if I give my
whole mind to a thing I am bound to succeed, dear Mother, in
the end, through steady application. Thus the battle within rages
more fiercely than ever. Sometimes I am foolhardy, and confident
in my own tenacity; at others, doubtful, when I think of the
immense stretch of road before me which I might by this time
have covered. As for [Anton] Thibaut,* he has long been advising
me to take up music. I should be very glad if you would write to
him, and I know he would be pleased. He went to Rome some
time ago, so I shall not have another chance of seeing him.

If I keep to law it certainly means spending another winter here
to attend Thibaut's lectures on the Pandects, which no law student
can afford to miss. If I decide on music, I must as certainly leave
here and return to Leipzig. I should be quite glad to go under
Wieck, who knows me, and can gauge my capabilities. Later
on I should want a year in Vienna, and, if possible, lessons from
Moscheles. And now dear Mother, one request, which you will
perhaps be glad to fulfil. *Will you write yourself to Wieck at Leipzig,*

---

*Schumann's law professor in Heidelberg.

and ask him plainly what he thinks of me and my scheme? Please let me have a speedy reply, telling me your decision, so that I can hasten my departure from Heidelberg, loath as I am to leave this paradise, my many friends and my bright dreams. Enclose this letter in your own to Wieck, if you like. In any case the matter must be settled by Michaelmas; then I will work, vigorously and without regrets, at my chosen profession.

You will admit that this is the most important letter I have ever written, or am likely to write. I hope you will not mind doing what I ask. Please answer as soon as possible; there is no time to be lost. Farewell, my dear Mother, and do not be anxious. It is a clear case of 'Heaven helps those who help themselves,' you see.

'I HAVE DECIDED ON A JOURNEY TO, AND A SOJOURN AT, SOME PLACE ABROAD, WHICH, THROUGH FURNISHING THE FINEST MODELS IN ART, WOULD PROVE TO ME OF THE GREATEST PROFIT'

JENNY LIND FLIES THE NEST

In 1841, the promising young operatic singer Jenny Lind (1820–87) was faced with a difficult decision.

Ever since she had graced the stage at only ten years old, Lind's entrancing voice and musical skill well beyond her years had been serenading audiences across Sweden. She forged a reputation as Sweden's brightest star in the National Drama, and was the nation's darling as the court singer of the ruling king, Carl Johan. At 20 years old, however, she felt restless, sensing that she was quickly outgrowing her domestic setting.

Eager to keep her on home soil, the Royal Theatre in Stockholm presented Lind with a renewed contract which they hoped would entice the young starlet to remain in Sweden. Though agreeable in every respect, the offer failed to sway Lind from her determination to reach new heights as a performer. Realizing it was time to fly the nest, Lind submitted this humble letter of rejection to the Royal

Theatre, laying out her designs for pursuing her musical future among the great institutions of Europe.

Her decision to leave Sweden proved a pivotal moment in her career. Indeed, had she left the decision any longer, it may have been too late. In the same year as she sent this letter, Lind travelled to France to come under the tutelage of singing teacher Signor Manuel García at the prestigious Paris Conservatory. Their first meeting could not have gone worse, with García deeming Lind's voice to have been irrevocably damaged by years of poor management and over-exertion during her time singing in Sweden. Lind, however, refused to be dismissed outright, and pleaded with García for a solution. His prescription: six weeks of complete and utter silence. Only then might he have something to work with.

Lind followed García's prescription to the letter, filling her time learning the languages of opera (Italian and French), and after six weeks her voice was restored to a point from which it could be rebuilt. From this moment on, Lind was unstoppable.

Word of her captivating voice soon spread, and she toured all over Europe, even performing in front of Queen Victoria on her English debut in 1847 at Her Majesty's Theatre. In 1850 she achieved global fame when she embarked on an incredibly successful tour of the United States, where she performed over 150 concerts all across the continent. Such was the power of her voice that she came to be known as the 'Swedish Nightingale'.

JENNY LIND, C. 1850

From Jenny Lind to the Directors of the Royal Theatre

1841

In reply to the letter from the Directors of the Royal Theatre, dated 15th December last year, I have the honour to state as follows: The musical and dramatic capabilities, which, from my earliest years, I have felt myself to possess, have, thanks to the cultivation received at home, though hitherto insufficient, still been able to attract some attention to my dawning talent; but it is not with half developed, if even happy, natural gifts that an artist can keep his ground; and, greatly as I prize the appreciation I have been fortunate enough already to win, I feel I ought to consider it not so much a homage to the artist I was and am, as an encouragement to what I might become.

With this conviction and in order to attain the artistic perfection open to me, I have thought it a duty to do what I can, and not to draw back before any sacrifice, either of youth, health, comfort or labour, not to speak of the modest sum I have managed to save, in the hope of reaching what may, perhaps, prove an unattainable aim. In consequence I have decided on a journey to, and a sojourn at, some place abroad, which, through furnishing the finest models in art, would prove to me of the greatest profit.

It is, then, chiefly this journey which constitutes the real obstacle to my immediately accepting, in its entirety, the kind offer of the Directors of the Royal Theatre; for it defers, for another year, the possibility of my re-engagement. I am in hopes, however, that the Royal Directors will not disapprove of my resolution, all the more as it aims solely at perfecting myself in my art; while all sacrifices, inseparable from a similar undertaking, will fall on myself alone. Trusting that the Royal Directors will accord to these reasons due consideration, and, in accordance with the request made in their kind letter, I beg leave to submit my counter proposals.

On returning to my native country, next year, I undertake to serve at the Royal Theatre for the two following years at the salary proposed by the Royal Directors in the above-mentioned letter of the 15th December last, but with the following modifications; that my engagement, for each year, may not exceed eight months, viz., from 1st October unto the following 31st May, so that a leave of the four months, June, July, August and September may be accorded to me.

Furthermore, I must, rather as a humble petition, than as a condition for my return to the service of the Royal Theatre, express my wish to be free this year from next 31st May, since in the beginning of June an opportunity offers for me to start on my intended journey in company with a family without whose protection I should not venture to undertake it. I hope the Royal Directors will, kindly, give due weight to this invaluable advantage, and, in view of its importance to me, excuse my earnest request.

Jenny Lind

Stockholm, 9 February, 1841

'IT IS MY OPINION THAT MUSIC AS AN ART IN ENGLAND WILL GO TO THE DEVIL VERY SOON IF SOME . . . CAPABLE YOUNG EDUCATED MUSICIANS DO NOT TAKE IT IN HAND'

ARTHUR SULLIVAN AND THE EFFORT TO SAVE ENGLISH MUSIC

To gain a better perspective on one's own culture, it is often necessary to experience that of other nations. Removing oneself from the home environment can enable one to look back, as it were, on one's own society from an external vantage point, and develop in turn a renewed understanding of the peculiar norms, traits and conventions which dictate one's native society. It is from such a vantage point that a young Arthur Sullivan formed his diagnosis of the issues afflicting the art music tradition in England in 1860. To these artistic ailments, moreover, Sullivan was certain, *he* would serve as the antidote.

Sullivan (1842–1900) heard his musical calling from an early age, producing his first composition at the age of eight, and publishing his first piece *'O Israel'* at the age of 13. A year later he became the first recipient of the Mendelssohn Scholarship from the Royal Academy of Music, an award granting him a year's study at the academy. So impressive was his progress that the grant was renewed twice, with the third award allowing him to continue his education in Germany at the world-renowned Leipzig Conservatoire.

Sullivan's time in Germany proved to be an important episode in his development as a musician. Not only did it give him the opportunity to train with many of the great European composers, including Julius Rietz, Carl Reinecke, Moritz Hauptmann and Ignaz Moscheles, but it was also during this time that Sullivan's passion for conducting began to form. So sure was he of his skill in this discipline that he began to consider what he could do to revive the art of conducting back home. Sullivan was convinced that the musical environment had grown stagnant in England and, driven by a deep sense of patriotism, he decided it was his duty to reverse this downward trend.

It was a belief he made clear in a letter to his mother on 31 October 1860. Interestingly, Sullivan's criticisms fall not only on the quality of English conductors, but on English audiences also. With a healthy dose of youthful arrogance, Sullivan suggested to his mother that audiences back home lack the discerning ear to even know what good music is. Still, he thought there were unique qualities to English orchestras, and it was these he intended to champion on his return home.

As it would turn out, Sullivan's approach to conducting would receive mixed reviews from critics, with some deeming his highly controlled style to lack the vigour and drama they had come to expect. This style only came to be accentuated when, on account of kidney stones, Sullivan took to conducting from an armchair. Others, however, were more receptive to his conservative approach, and Sullivan enjoyed a long career conducting orchestras across Britain at such prestigious events as the Glasgow Choral Union concerts and Leeds Music Festival.

From Arthur Sullivan to his mother, Mary Clementina Coghlan, 1860

31 October 1860

Mother, my great hobby is still conducting. I have been told by many of the masters here that I was born to be a conductor and consequently have been educating myself to a high degree in that branch of the art. If I can only once obtain an opportunity to show what I can do in that way I feel confident of my success afterwards. Do not mistake this for conceit . . . but I am getting of an age now when I shall be obliged to have confidence in myself and my own resources. I often try to think what would have become of me had I never come to Germany. In England there was very little more for me to learn. I had heard and knew well almost all the small stock of music which is ever performed in London (and it is *very* little compared to what one hears here). I should have made very little improvement in pianoforte playing, whereas now thanks to Messrs Moscheles and Plaidy, I am a tolerably decent player . . . Besides increasing and maturing my judgement of music it has taught me how good works ought to be done. They have no idea in England of making the orchestras play with that degree of light and shade to which they have attained here, and that is what I aim at – to bring the English orchestra to the same perfection as the Continental ones, and to even still greater, for the power and tone of ours are much greater than the foreign . . .

If something does not please them (tickle their ears) the first time they hear it they throw it aside and will not have anything more to do with it, forgetting that really good music is seldom appreciated by one the first time of hearing, but that it grows on one and one sees its beauties gradually. Take Beethoven, for instance. His fifth symphony was poohpooh'd [*sic*] and laughed at when it was first tried at the Philharmonic; Carl M. von Weber said of his eighth (or seventh) that the composer was fit for the madhouse. The Choral Symphony is only just now beginning to be *understood* in England. And yet what do we think of Beethoven now? Suppose they had cast him aside, as they do Schumann (the most popular German composer), Schubert, Gade, and other less distinguished composers. Look at the programme for tomorrow night's concert . . . Fancy seeing Schumann and Wagner in the same programme in England. The time will come yet I hope . . .

The fact is I am letting out now all the rage which has been concentrated in me ever since I began reading that wretched *Musical*

World. It is my opinion that music as an art in England will go to the devil very soon if some few enthusiastic, practical and capable young educated musicians do not take it in hand. I get so savage sometimes when in company here and talking to great artists who have been to England at the sneering way in which they talk of 'England's art', English taste . . . and yet I ought not to be angry with them for I feel that they are quite right. However, hope and persevere is my motto . . .

ARTHUR SULLIVAN WRITING, C. 1900

'A HUSBAND AND WIFE WHO ARE BOTH COMPOSERS . . . DO YOU HAVE ANY IDEA HOW RIDICULOUS IT WOULD APPEAR . . .?'

GUSTAV MAHLER'S MARRIAGE CONDITIONS

In December 1901, the composers Gustav Mahler (1860–1911) and Alma Schindler (1879–1964) were making the final arrangements for their wedding. The couple had only met one month earlier, but their infatuation with one another was so intense that they decided they *had* to be married as soon as possible. Before they could tie the knot, however, Gustav felt there was one matter that needed to be clarified for them to become partners in marriage. It was an issue he had been anxious to confront and, while away in Dresden, he took the opportunity to send this now infamous letter to his betrothed, laying down in no uncertain terms the ground rules for their marriage.

Across 20 pages, Gustav explained in laborious detail his one clear demand: if he and Alma were to be wed, then their nuptials must also mark the end of her career as a composer. Though he professed not to adhere to ideals of male supremacy, he was an adamant defender of the traditional conventions of marriage, which were not, he concluded, compatible with his betrothed's career.

In her memoir, Alma recalled that she had attempted her first composition at only eight years old. Her passion for music developed under the tutelage of Josef Labor and Alexander von Zemlinsky, the latter's coinciding, and ending, with her engagement to Gustav. Before her marriage Alma had composed some 20 piano pieces and a few pieces of chamber music. Though only one collection of songs had actually been published prior to her engagement, Gustav still felt that his future bride had to give up composition to be able to dedicate herself completely to the duties of a wife, mother and muse.

In return, he promised to be the family's sole provider, funding their upkeep through *his* compositions. It is undisputable that Gustav was a talented composer: by the time of their betrothal he was already a famous musician and had composed world-famous

Romantic symphonies which thousands flocked to see him conduct on his celebrated 'first nights'. But this was no easy demand to make of his future wife, and Alma – who was never short of romantic prospects – must have weighed her options carefully before deciding to accept Gustav's terms; the couple were married on 9 March 1902.

The couple's marriage was cut short by Gustav's premature death in 1911. Alma outlived him by over 50 years, and in her own memoir and biographies of her late husband she took a heavy hand to the narratives surrounding their marriage. For years she was viewed as the primary source of information as to the character and life of Gustav Mahler; in the years following her death, however, it was discovered that Alma had somewhat skewed this history by withholding and editing key primary sources – notably Gustav's letters. Such was the confusion that historians have come to refer to 'the Alma Problem', and many letters, including this one, continue to plague music scholars hoping to determine the true nature of the relationship: affectionate, controlling, or generous measures of both?

GUSTAV MAHLER, C. 1911

From Gustav Mahler to Alma Schindler, 1901

19 December 1901

Dresden
Hotel Bellevue

My dearest Almschi,

Today, my beloved Alma, it is with a heavy heart that I set out to write this letter. I know I must hurt you, but I have no choice . . . If we are to be happy together, there is one particular aspect of our relationship that we must discuss and clarify for now and ever more, for it is the very basis of our bond.

Admittedly I am reading between the lines of yesterday's letter . . . at the time, you wrote: I want to be all you <u>need</u> and <u>wish for</u>. Those words made me profoundly happy, they filled me with blissful trust. But now, perhaps without realizing it, you have revoked them . . .

In your letter, you write of 'your' music' and 'my' music. <u>Forgive me, but I cannot remain silent!</u> . . . From now on, would you be able to regard <u>my</u> music as if it were <u>your own</u>? . . . A husband and wife who are both composers: how do you envisage that? Such a strange relationship between rivals: do you have any idea how ridiculous it would appear, can you imagine the loss of self-respect it would later cause us both? If, at a time when you should be attending to household duties or fetching me something I urgently need, or if, as you wrote, you wish to relieve me of life's trivia – if at such a moment you were befallen by 'inspiration': what then? . . . one thing is certain: if we are to be happy together, you will have to be 'as I need you' – not my colleague, but my wife! If you were to abandon <u>your</u> music in order to take possession of mine, and also to be mine: would this signify the end of life as you know it, and if you did so, would you feel you were renouncing a higher existence?

Before we can think of forging a bond for life, we <u>must</u> agree on this question. What do you mean when you write: 'I haven't worked any more – since then!' 'Now I have to return to my work' etc. etc.?

What kind of work is this? Composition? Do you compose for your own pleasure or for the benefit of mankind?

. . . As I said, this has nothing to do with your compositions, for I don't even know them; this is about your attitude towards me and its essence, which will determine the future of our life together...

But from now on you have only <u>one</u> profession: <u>to make me happy!</u> Do you understand, Alma? I do realize that if you are to make me happy, you yourself must be happy (on my account). But in this drama, which could develop equally well into a comedy or a tragedy (both of which would be inappropriate), the roles must be correctly cast. The role of the 'composer', the 'bread-winner', is mine; yours is that of the loving partner, the sympathetic comrade. Are you satisfied with it? . . .

This letter will come as a dreadful shock to you – I know it, Alma, and even if this is only cold comfort, you can well imagine that I am suffering just as much . . . this is a moment of great importance, these are decisions that will weld two people together for eternity. I bless you, my dearest, my love, no matter how you react . . . Many tender kisses, my Alma. And I beg you: be truthful! Your Gustav

'I PRACTISED 6 HOURS A DAY. NOW THAT'S <u>HARD LABOR</u>'

ZITKÁLA-ŠÁ'S THIRST FOR A MUSICAL EDUCATION

Zitkála-Šá, also known as Gertrude Simmons Bonnin (1876–1938), was a highly skilled writer, political activist, musical educator and translator. She was heavily involved in fighting for the rights of Native American peoples, and in 1926 one of the co-founders of the National Council of American Indians. On top of her work as a political reformer, Zitkála-Šá was a keen musician and studied at the New England Conservatory of Music at the end of the nineteenth century.

Looking to put her knowledge to good use, Zitkála-Šá took a teaching job in Pennsylvania in 1899 teaching Native American children to play music. Later in 1910, Zitkála-Šá wrote the libretto for *The Sun Dance Opera* with the composer William Hanson, which was lauded as the first Native American opera, premiering in 1913.

Determined to engross herself in music as much as possible, Zitkála-Šá also began learning the piano – a considerable 'hard labour' that she detailed in a letter to her friend Carlos Montezuma. Her excitement to study a particularly challenging piano piece only underscores her talent and determination, all the more so when considered alongside her decision to send her son away to school where he too can receive a good education, even if it means having to leave him for long, difficult periods. Her aspiration to earn a diploma in piano music stands as a testament to her perseverance and ambition. Zitkála-Šá's pursuit of knowledge and artistic expression is particularly significant in the context of her identity as a Native American woman breaking down barriers in a largely Eurocentric field.

ZITKÁLA-ŠÁ PHOTOGRAPHED WITH HER VIOLIN, 1898

From Zitkála-Šá to Carlos Montezuma, 1913

June 23rd 1913

My dear Dr Montezuma —

Time got away so fast that I am taking a wait here for a few letters among which is one to you. I am bound for Spalding Institute for Small Boys — a Benedictine Sisters School — Nauvoo, Ill — The nearest railroad station is across the river at Montrose, Iowa. I will arrive there at 8 p.m. tonight. I am taking my boy to school. I know it is necessary to educate him but this knowledge does not make it any easier to <u>leave</u> him . . .

While in Westerville I had my eyes examined — you know what that means. Oh — no — I was not thinking of old age — I mean — the Belladona used to enlarge the pupils of the eyes — I could not use my eyes for ten days or more! Then when I recovered — for I was sick incidentally from a severe cold contracted while in Chicago — I studied piano music at Otterbein University. I practised 6 hours a day. Now that's <u>hard labor</u>. I want to earn a diploma in Piano Music one of these days. You know I have a great desire to finish things I had once started — (I have no table to write on so excuse very poor writing) I studied a piano piece which is considered one of the most difficult things written for the piano. Prof Grahill said I had talent. I am not bragging but simply telling you the encouragement I have along my line of study.

I am returning to Utah because Mr Bonnin insists upon it. I shall continue my study at home and try to go every summer to some place to study under a real first class teacher of music. I am telling you all this because I want you to know that I intend to improve my mind — I intend also to direct my boy's course in school — hence forth . . .

Yours sincerely

Gertrude Bonnin

'I UNDERSTAND YOUR FEARS AT MY COMING HERE . . . BUT I REALLY DO THINK THERE'S AN AWFULLY GOOD CHANCE I WON'T BLOW IT THIS TIME'

THE TRIALS AND TRIBULATIONS OF JANIS JOPLIN'S QUEST FOR SUCCESS

Surprise, confusion, and perhaps concern – these were likely to be the emotions racing through Janis Joplin's parents' minds when they opened a letter from their daughter and discovered it had been posted from San Francisco. As far as they had been aware, Joplin (1943–70) had left the family home for Austin, Texas, where she would play music in local bars as she waited for school to begin again. Joplin may have intended to follow through with this plan, but news reached her of an opportunity out west in San Francisco that she just couldn't resist. While she departed for California full of hope and dreams, her anxious parents were left with the reminder of how her first trip to the city had ended.

As a child growing up in Texas, Joplin had failed to fit the mould of what was deemed 'normal'. She had struggled to fit in at school, where her eccentric manner attracted unwanted attention from bullies. In music, though, she found a refuge, and she spent much of her time listening to the blues, folk and rock 'n' roll records her other 'misfit' friends introduced her to.

Joplin knew she needed to get out of the state, and in 1963 she decided to quit her studies at the University of Texas and hitchhike with her friend and future promoter, Chet Helms, the 1,700 miles to San Francisco. The city was at this time the heart of the emerging hippie movement, and Joplin travelled there with dreams of stardom. To begin with, she made great strides, impressing all she met with her incredible husky voice. A breakthrough was slow to emerge, however, and slowly Joplin became embroiled in the darker side of the city's free-spirited hedonism. By 1965 she had developed a serious drug and alcohol problem, and it became clear that she needed to break the cycle of her hectic lifestyle and return home.

Once home, Joplin was soon back on her feet and, much to her parents' approval, decided to go back to school. Nevertheless, a life in music lay ever in the back of her mind, and within a year she was being coaxed back to the West Coast. The call had come from her friend Helms, who wanted Joplin to join the band he was managing called Big Brother and the Holding Co., that was in need of a singer. Helms thought Joplin's bluesy style would be the perfect fit. It was an opportunity Joplin simply could not pass up, and she resolved it would be the fresh start she needed in her quest for stardom.

Still, Joplin must have known how her sudden flight west would affect her parents, and her remorse at the deceit – intentional or otherwise – is evident in her confessional letter. Soon Joplin's risk would prove fruitful, as Big Brother and the Holding Co. rose to the forefront of the San Francisco music scene, and Joplin herself went on to soar higher and higher.

JANIS JOPLIN, C. 1966–70

From Janis Joplin to Dorothy and Seth Joplin, 1966

6 June 1966

Mother & Dad . . .

With a great deal of trepidation, I bring the news. I'm in San Francisco. Now let me explain – when I got to Austin, I talked to Travis Rivers who gave me a spiel about my singing w/a band out here. Seems Chet Helms, old friend, now is Mr Big in S.F. Owns 3 big *working* Rock & roll bands with bizarre names like Captain Beefheart & his Magic Band, Big Brother & the Holding Co. etc. Well, Big Brother et al needs a vocalist. So I called Chet to talk to him about it. He encouraged me to come out – seems the whole city had gone rock & roll (and it has!) and assured me fame & fortune. I told him I was worried about being hung up out here w/no way back & he agreed to furnish me w/a bus ticket back home if I did just come & try. So I came.

Had a nice trip – camped out at night along the Rio Grande, collected rocks, etc. now I'm staying w/some old friends from Austin, Kit and Margo Teele – he works for Dun & Bradstreet, she for the telephone co.

I don't really know what's happening yet. Supposed to rehearse w/the band this afternoon, after that I guess I'll know whether I want to stay & do that for awhile. Right now my position is ambivalent – I'm glad I came, nice to see the city, a few friends, but I'm not at all sold on the idea of becoming the poor man's Cher. So I guess we'll see.

I just want to tell you that I *am* trying to keep a level head about everything & not go overboard w/enthusiasm. I'm sure you're both convinced my self-destructive streak has won out again but I'm really trying. I do plan on coming back to school – unless, I must admit, this turns into a good thing. Chet is a very important man out here now & he wanted *me* specifically, to sing w/this band. I haven't tried yet so I can't say what I'm going to do – so far I'm safe, well fed, and nothing has been stolen.

I suppose you could write me at this address although I don't know how long I'll be here. I expected a letter from Linda – Maybe John – if they've arrived, please send them also. The address is c/o C. L. Teele, 23rd St., S.F.

I'm awfully sorry to be such a disappointment to you. I understand your fears at my coming here & must admit I share them, but I really do think there's an awfully good chance I won't blow it this time. There's really nothing more I can say now. Guess I'll write more when I have more news, until then, address all criticism to the above address. And please believe that you can't possibly want for me to be a winner more than I do.

Love, Janis

Will write a long happy & enthusiastic letter as soon as I stop feeling guilty. My love to Mike & Laura. Want to write Laura & tell her about the dances – FANTASTIC! And the clothes & people. Will in due time.

I love you, I'm sorry . . .

'THE BAND HAVE NOW BROKEN UP DUE MAINLY TO . . . PARANOIA & SPITE'

ANARCHY IN THE BAND: JOHNNY ROTTEN EXPLAINS THE SEX PISTOLS' BREAK-UP

By the end of 1977, the Sex Pistols had risen to become the most notorious punk band in Britain. Their singles 'Anarchy in the UK' and 'God Save the Queen' had taken the nation's youth by storm, and the album *Never Mind the Bollocks* (released in October that year) had debuted at number one in the UK album charts. Such heights of fame brought with it a surge of fan mail, much of which was addressed to the band's occasionally volatile lead singer, John Lydon, known then as 'Johnny Rotten' (b. 1956).

Usually much of this fan mail would go unanswered, but in the case of a letter sent by one Martin Smyth, a 12-year-old boy from Belfast, Lydon made an exception. The reply was not of the nature that Smyth might have expected, however, for in it Lydon personally broke the news that he was no longer a member of the Sex Pistols. While this may have been a great shock to the young fan, when one looks at the madness that surrounded the band it is surprising they managed to last as long as they did.

The original lineup of the Sex Pistols lasted only three years, between 1975 and 1977. In that limited time the band managed to achieve a level of celebrity infamy almost unprecedented, which left a lasting impression on the national psyche. They were deemed of such ill taste that the BBC decided to ban them, and to get booked they often had to tour under a pseudonym.

The chaotic outward image of the band was reflected also in the fractious relationships within it. In 1977, Sid Vicious was brought into the band after the original bassist Glen Matlock was reportedly chucked out, and almost from the very beginning there was an uneasy relationship between Lydon and lead guitarist Steve Jones. At the root of most of the band's problems, however, was their manager, Malcolm McLaren. It was he who had masterminded much of the Pistols' success, he and his girlfriend, the world-renowned designer Vivian Westwood, who had cultivated the Pistols' iconic punk image – and he who orchestrated their most outrageous moments, including the band's calamitous protest at the monarch's Silver Jubilee by sailing down the River Thames playing their hit single 'God Save the Queen'.

While McLaren knew how to pull off a publicity stunt, however, he was less effective as a manager, and Lydon become increasingly frustrated with his mismanagement of the band, eventually deciding to make his exit in early 1978 during their disastrous debut tour of the United States.

JOHNNY ROTTEN IN THE SEX PISTOLS' US DEBUT, 1978

From Johnny Rotten to Martin Smyth, 1978

Dear Martin,

I received your letter the other day from Virgin and decided to reply to you personally cos it's not the usual type of letter that I get sent. Mostly there [*sic*] from silly girls who've fallen in love and want to marry me, or just plain mad death threats. So . . .

The band have now broken up due mainly to Mr McLaren's paranoia & spite. Steve and Paul's foolishness for still believing he ain't no crook, and Sid's stupid drug abuse. I ain't totally without blame either I suppose, cos I freely admit to being an arrogant big head who always has a sarcastic answer when I feel like it.

However all that has past now, and we, or at least I will not work with them ever again. The future or lack of it ain't [*sic*] so dim, Malcolm will find someone new to abuse and steal from when he's finished spending Paul and Steve's money in Rio. They'll always be told what to do. Sid I hope will grow up and give up his stupid weakness, and I'm going solo. I've already recorded several new songs, but since Malcolm will not come back to London I cannot release them, because the old contracts have not yet been terminated (he's well aware of this by the way and I've had to get a lawyer on to it.)

Never mind though, life's still fun, just about.

Ta for writing & sorry I can't give my address for obvious reasons, but if you want to write again for anything just send it to Virgin and I'll get it.

Yours

John Rotten

PS The rest of the band are either in Rio or [illegible]. I think, cos I haven't seen or heard from them since.

'REMEMBER THAT ROMANTIC SAYING, "I WOULD DIE FOR YOU"? WELL, I NEARLY DID'

ELTON JOHN BIDS FAREWELL TO COCAINE

On 10 August 1990, Elton John decided it was time to part ways with an old companion. They had been acquainted since the 1970s, and had shared many wild and memorable moments together. In fact, there had rarely been a time when the two weren't together. Even when John (b. 1947) longed for solitude, his friend always seemed to find a way to keep them together. After nearly three decades within this intense and intimate relationship, John knew he had reached his limit, and took up his pen to write a farewell letter. There would be no expectation of a response, nor any chance of reprieve, for this letter was not addressed to any ex-band member or lover. Instead, the letter was intended for one of the most addictive and destructive drugs known to man – cocaine.

Elton John had struggled with cocaine addiction for the best part of his career. When he should have been enjoying the fruits of his success as one of the bestselling pop stars of all time, he instead found himself alone and isolated from the ones who truly loved him. These self-destructive tendencies reached breaking point in

1990, and John finally resolved to check himself into rehab to kick the habit that had on several occasions nearly taken his life.

As part of his treatment John was encouraged to perform the cathartic exercise of confronting his demons via the medium of letters. One such letter was the one he addressed to cocaine itself, personified here as an ex-lover. Thankfully, John managed to work through his addiction, and was able to get back to what he truly loved: writing and performing music, which he continued to do right up until 2023, culminating in his mammoth, five-year farewell tour, 'Farewell Yellow Brick Road'.

ELTON JOHN PERFORMS A SONG AT THE PIANO, C. 1984

From Elton John to 'cocaine', 1990

Lutheran Hospital,
Park Ridge,
Illinois

10 August 1990

We've lived together, you and I, for sixteen years, and boy, have we had some great times. But now it's time for me to sit down and tell you how I really feel about you. I loved you so much. At first, we were inseparable – we seemed to meet so often, either at my house, or at other people's. In the end, we were so fond of each other that I decided I couldn't be without you. I wanted us to be a great couple and to hell with what other people thought.

When I first met you, you seemed to bring out everything that had been suppressed before. I could talk about anything I wanted for the first time in my life. There was something in your make-up that brought all my walls and barriers crashing down. You made me feel free. I was never jealous if other people shared you. In fact, I liked turning other people on to your charms. I realize how stupid I must have been, because you never really cared for me. It was all one-sided. You only care about how many people you can trap in your web.

My body and brain have suffered greatly because of my love for you – you have left me with permanent physical and mental scars. Remember that romantic saying, 'I would die for you'? Well, I nearly did. Still, you're a hard lady to get rid of. We've split so many times before but I always went back to you. Even though I knew it was a mistake, I still did. When there was no-one else to comfort me, you were only a phone call away at any hour of the day or night. You never cease to amaze me – I've sent cars to pick you up and I even sent planes so that you and I could spend some hours or days together. And when you finally arrived, I was ecstatic to embrace you once more.

We had great parties with people. We had great, intense talks about how we were going to change the world. Of course, we never did, but boy, could we talk! We had sex with people we barely knew and who we really didn't give a damn about. I didn't care who they were as long as they slept with me. But, in the morning, they were gone, and I was alone again. You had gone too. Sometimes I wanted you so insatiably, but you had vanished. With you by my side, I was all-conquering, but with you gone I was just a sad little child again.

My family never liked you at all. In fact, they hated the spell you had me under. You managed to push me away from them and lots of my friends. I wanted them to understand how I felt about you, but they never listened, and I would feel anger, and hurt. I felt ashamed because I cared more about you than I did about my own flesh and blood. All I cared about was myself and you. So I kept you to myself. In the end, I didn't want to share you anymore. I just wanted us to be alone. I became more miserable, because you ruled my life – you were my Svengali.

I guess I'll try and come to the point of this letter. It's taken me sixteen years to realize that you've taken me nowhere. Whenever I tried to have a relationship with someone else, I always brought you along at some point. So I have no doubts that it was me who was the user. But I found no compassion and love – what love I had for anyone was always superficial.

I had grown tired and hateful towards myself, but recently, I met someone again – someone I loved and trusted, and that person was adamant that this was going to be a two-way love affair, not a three-way one. He made me realize how self-centred I had become, and he made me think about my life and my sense of values. My life has ground to a halt. I now have the opportunity to change my way of living and thinking. I am prepared to accept humility, and therefore have to say goodbye to you for the final time.

You have been my whore. You have kept me from any sort of spirituality and you have kept me from finding out who I really am. I don't want you and I to share the same grave. I want to die a natural death when I go, at peace with myself. I want to live the rest of my life being honest and facing the consequences rather than hiding behind my celebrity status. I feel as though, after sixteen years with you, I was dead anyway. Once more, white lady – goodbye. If I run into you somewhere – and, let's face it, you're such a woman about town – I'll ignore you and leave immediately. You've seen me enough over the years and I'm sick of you. You've won the fight – I surrender.

Thanks but no thanks,

Elton

CHAPTER SEVEN

THE HEARTBEAT OF SOCIETY

'Go to your record collection and mind-erase those who have led questionable lives and see how much of it remains,' writes Nick Cave in his superb meditation on the decline of modern rock music articulated as a letter to 'Dylan and Jason' in 2019 and reproduced in this chapter. The letter in its entirety is a thundering denunciation of the 'moral zealotry' Cave sees as afflicting culture and society alike, and a clarion call for the return of the kinds of transgression and subversion that defined the rock 'n' roll of the past. 'Art must be wrestled from the hands of the pious, in whatever form they come,' he concludes: 'and they are always coming, knives out, intent on murdering creativity.'

Cave's is a letter about rock 'n' roll; and he prescribes destruction such that out of its ashes can rise a revitalized artform, truer to its transgressive self. But it is also a letter which – sometimes explicitly, sometimes implicitly – addresses society itself, musing on the nature of the relationship of art and artists with the world in which they exist, which they depict, and with which they enter into dialogue. If 'art' is anything at all then it is surely, most fundamentally, an interaction with the world as its creator finds it: a struggle to create meaning out of meaninglessness.

Alone on our tiny chunk of rock, our mere speck of dust floating in the vast, inky nothingness of space, we have throughout our history as a species found art – found music – to be the way in which we *express*, and through which we inch our way towards an understanding of what it is to be human. As we have done so, our utterly innate human impulse to strive for the 'next' has directed our gaze outwards; out into that inky nothingness. And so our questions about meaning and understanding have grown more complex as we consider them not just in isolation but also in the context of how we could – maybe indeed how we will – relate to other life forms. It should be no surprise, then, that NASA chose the best way we have yet found of expressing ourselves, of understanding ourselves, to load onto the Voyager spacecraft and launch into space in 1977. On a specially curated and designed 'Golden Record' there are represented musical traditions from across the globe – all of which are still hurtling through the universe, and now some 15 billion miles from Earth. It is difficult to imagine what another life-form would make of Chuck Berry's 'Johnny B. Goode', or of Bach's *Well-Tempered Clavier*, or of Javanese Gamelan. But the decision to make this record and offer it up as the best – most *meaningful* – creation of our species tells us a lot about ourselves.

Music is, then, as this chapter's title suggests, the heartbeat of society. Some letters in it brilliantly illustrate the influence music has or is perceived to have by those – perhaps Cave's 'puritans'? – concerned with moral standards. Perhaps most striking, though, is the letter from the American composer John Donald Robb to Frank Colapinto towards the end of the Second World War, in which he muses on the question, 'What should post-war music be like?'

War begets a musical response: it has always been so. If music is humanity's way of understanding itself, then so much greater are the demands placed upon it when the understanding sought is of humanity's destruction of itself. Robb's evaluation of the musical response to the Great War is that it traced the world's impulse to '[seek] salvation in something new', resulting in music which, in his view, was too much the product of 'revolutionary intellectualism.'

'Composers have been composing for composers, critics and conductors,' he observes, 'and the public has reacted by demanding less of this "modern" music in our concert halls or by turning to popular music — a field in which oddly enough conservatism has prevailed.'

In general terms Robb's argument is persuasive, but it is interesting to note that the modernist turn was never much in evidence in England. Perhaps the English are uniquely nostalgic — uniquely prelapsarian in their outlook — but the musical response to the Great War in England was largely one of a reaching back to an (imaginary?) age of innocence, and of the infusion of that innocence with a restrained, dignified melancholy. Indeed, there is an argument that the modernist turn in art music was driven by composers who belonged to nations coming to terms with defeat, not victory — where 'salvation in something new' was the only option in response to the old having been swept aside.

If it is true, as Robb writes, that 'the mind could not create great music without the heart,' then we must be content to understand music, at least in part, as the outward expression of a heartbeat, individual and societal. And so salvation is sought in the new by those for whom the old has crumbled to dust; while the victorious are left to survey their empty villages and ask, 'but at what cost?' Both these responses, to disagree with Robb's inherent value judgement, are interpretations of that heartbeat. And when our own, individual resolve falters — when the steady beating drum of our own heartbeat flickers and fluctuates — we turn, so often, to music. 'Our lives are spent in drunken orgies and parachute descents to escape shelling or Bosch aeroplanes,' writes J. Lawrence Fry to Edward Elgar from the trenches of the Great War. 'In fact the whole thing is unreal, and music is all that we have to help us carry on.'

'MUSIC – BEING IDENTICAL WITH HEAVEN – ISN'T A THING OF MOMENTARY THRILLS OR EVEN HOURLY ONES. IT'S A CONDITION OF ETERNITY'

A FESTIVAL OF MUSIC: GUSTAV HOLST RECOUNTS THE WHITSUNTIDE CELEBRATIONS AT THAXTED

In 1913 Gustav Holst, a composer famous for his celestial suite *The Planets*, found himself in the picturesque north Essex village of Thaxted. He had stumbled across the village while out on one of his much-loved rambles, and from the moment he set eyes on the 181-foot spire of the town's church, he was utterly enamoured. Holst (1874–1934) bought a cottage in the village later that year, and would stay in the village until 1925. Over this time, Thaxted became more than just a refuge in which Holst could compose. It formed the heart of his public life, and his interaction with the local community served to stimulate him musically in more ways than he could imagine.

While composing was Holst's great passion, writing music alone seldom provided him with a sufficient income on which to live. Consequently further sources of income were required, and teaching became an important line of work. It was a profession he excelled in, and his aptitude for teaching stemmed in no small part from his strong belief in the need to democratize the arts.

Holst had become a member of the Socialist League while studying at the Royal College of Music, and during this time he conducted the Hammersmith Socialist Choir. He was also a keen supporter of the folk revival movement, the influences of which can be heard in such compositions as *A Somerset Rhapsody* (1906–7).

These egalitarian sympathies led Holst to become heavily involved with the local church choir in Thaxted, and before long plans for a Whitsuntide music festival were under way. The

festival was held in 1916, and drew together a collection of his
existing pupils as well as members of the local community. It was
a huge success, and the decision was made to make the festival an
annual event.

What Holst describes in this letter is nothing short of a musical
indulgence, as the whole town gives itself over to revelling
in the joy of music to the point of exhaustion. Writing to his
friend W. G. Whittaker, Holst extolled the virtues of playing
and composing music in all its forms. In turn, Holst reflected
critically on the relationship professional musicians have with their
music, arguing that they could learn something from the freedom
of expression found in folk and community music. It is not for
money that music should be played, but for the visceral emotional
experience it conjures – an experience which Holst here aligned
with entering Heaven.

GUSTAV HOLST, C. 1920

From Gustav Holst to W. G. Whittaker, 1917

June 4 [1917]

Dear W,

. . .

And now I want to try and write a little about Whitsuntide at Thaxted. How I wish you could come and realize it for yourself in 1918. For it must be released. One of the advantages of being over 40 is that one begins to learn the difference between knowing and realizing.

I realize now why the bible insists on heaven being a place (I should call it a condition) where people sing and <u>go on Singing</u>.

We kept it up at Thaxted about 14 hours a day. The reason why we didn't do more is that we were not capable mentally or physically of realizing heaven any further. Still as far as it went it was heaven. Just as the average amateur's way of using music as a sedative or stimulant is purgatory and the professional way of using music as a topic of conversation or as a means of money getting is hell.

Of course it's no use writing this. If you've had three days of perpetual music you've learnt it already if you haven't it's almost as sensible as describing the B minor to a deaf man.

Music – being identical with heaven – isn't a thing of momentary thrills or even hourly ones. It's a condition of eternity. As a girl in Thaxted said to me 'The great point of all this is that there is no reason why it should ever stop.' We had about 20 trebles 8 altos 2 tenors 3 basses 4 1st V 4 2nd 2 vlas [*sic*] 3 cellos one bass fl [*sic*] 2 ob [*sic*] 1 horn 1 local cornet and organ. We rehearsed Sat 6 to 9. We did enclosed program on Sunday morning and Monday morning, rather a longer one on Sunday evening.

Both afternoons we did odds and ends in church – Morleyite [*sic*] compositions, rounds, canons (the 8 part one in my 3d series with the 8 groups placed right round the church!) and also went round the village and serenaded people.

This was the official program. They filled in the intervals by singing and playing in church (where 'Sumer is icumen in' simply <u>grew</u> up from a group of people) in the houses, in gardens, on doorsteps (where I found 3 girls trying to sing the 8 pt round!) in the streets (the local policeman shut them up about 11 PM) and once on the church tower from whence they sang the Byrd Mass.

I arranged the three hymns for choir and orchestra. The whole district is singing 'The Church bells in Thaxted' now – it is almost as popular there as Bach's Sleepers Wake.

Morley concert next Sat – Wesley's 'Sing aloud' Parry's 'Glories of our blood and state' Locke's Macbeth the 2nd Vedas etc.

Yrs Ever,

GVH

. . .

'IN FACT THE WHOLE THING IS UNREAL, AND MUSIC IS ALL THAT WE HAVE TO HELP US CARRY ON'

AN OFFICER'S GRATITUDE FOR EDWARD ELGAR'S MUSIC
In 1877 Thomas Edison announced an invention which would mark the advent of a revolution in the way we listened to music. He called the new contraption the 'phonograph', and it allowed, for the first time, sound to be mechanically recorded then played back at will.

Other inquisitive minds soon latched onto the breakthrough to make further innovations in music technology; a key development in this regard came in 1887, when Emile Berliner invented the gramophone. Unlike Edison's phonograph, which worked by allowing the user to make home recordings on wax-coated cylinders, the gramophone relied on lateral-cut flat disc recordings. Such a feature meant the gramophone could only play pre-recorded discs, transforming the phonograph from a home-playback recording device into a music player.

It was at this point that the potential of remote music playing was truly realized, for from this moment on music was no longer the preserve of the musician; now it could be physically captured following a performance, ready to be reproduced outside the moment of its original playing.

For listeners, the gramophone brought yet unseen levels of agency in their music listening habits, allowing them to enjoy music whenever and wherever they wanted. It also democratized the world of music, opening the theatre and opera hall to those unable to attend performances in person.

The social impact of such new-found autonomy cannot be understated, for now the haven of music's beauty could be found in any setting or social situation. At the turn of the nineteenth century, in no place was this musical solace needed more than in the trenches of the First World War. This letter was sent by Captain Lawrence J. Fry to Edward Elgar in 1917 while he was trapped serving in the hellish chaos of the Western Front. Deprived of the comforts of the civilized world, Fry and his comrades found the gramophone the only thing that enabled them to transcend their horrific surroundings and escape – if just for a moment – to a world of music and peace.

The Starlight Express was a 1915 children's play adapted from Algernon Blackwood's novel *A Prisoner in Fairyland*, for which Edward Elgar composed the incidental music. The piece in question is the duet which rounds out the finale of Act III.

EDWARD ELGAR LEADS AN ORCHESTRA FOR A RECORDING
OF HIS MUSIC, 1914

From J. Lawrence Fry to Edward Elgar, 1917

5th October 1917

Dear Sir,

Though unknown, I feel I must write to you tonight. We possess a fairly good gramophone in our mess, and I have bought your record 'Starlight Express' "Hearts must be star-shiny dressed". It is being played for the twelfth time over. The Gramophone was Anathema to me before this War because it was abused so much. But all is changed now, and it is the only way of bringing back to us the days that are gone, and helping one through the Ivory gate that leads to fairy land or Heaven, whatever one likes to call it. And it is a curious thing, even those who only go for Rag-time Revues, all care for your music. Our lives are spent in drunken orgies and parachute descents to escape shelling or Bosch aeroplanes. In fact the whole thing is unreal, and music is all that we have to help us carry on. Sir Henry Miers of Manchester University. He will tell you all about me.

Yours sincerely

J Lawrence Fry
Captain
20th Balloon Section
RFC BEF

'WITHOUT MUSIC I SHOULD WISH TO DIE. EVEN POETRY, SWEET PATRON MUSE FORGIVE ME THE WORLDS, IS NOT WHAT MUSIC IS'

THE REJUVENATING FORCE OF MUSIC: EDNA ST VINCENT MILLAY FINDS SOLACE IN THE PIANO

For Edna St Vincent Millay, poetry was an artistic medium through which she could truly express herself. It was, as she describes here, her 'patron muse', and through it she became a defining voice of the Roaring Twenties. For all the joy she drew from this literary medium, however, it was not the only art form that resonated with her. In fact, as St Vincent Millay (1892–1950) here admits in a letter to the writer Allan Ross MacDougall, there had and always would be a unique quality to music that distinguished it as the supreme medium of expression. The relationship between the arts of music and poetry has long been a matter of searching debate within the arts, several examples of which feature across the letters in this collection. In this particular case of cross-pollination, we observe the deeply restorative relationship St Vincent Millay found with music.

Edna St Vincent Millay was a poet fascinated by the concept of beauty, and in music she found it in one of its purest forms. For her music was an art which could penetrate the soul like no other, and it was a theme which featured in many of her poems and sonnets, such as 'To a Musician', 'Dirge without Music' and 'West Country Song'. One composer for whose music she bore a particular fondness was Ludwig van Beethoven. Such was her passion that it even inspired her to write the poem 'On Hearing a Symphony of Beethoven', published in 1928, in which she explored the sheer beauty found in his compositions.

In this letter written eight years earlier we see a similar iteration of such emotion as Millay describes the rejuvenating influence of music, and most notably Beethoven's Fifth Symphony. In pieces such as this Millay could, for but a moment, recoil from the world, clear her mind and return to reality refreshed.

From Edna St Vincent Millay to Allan Ross MacDougall, 1920

77 West 12th Street,

New York City.
September 11th. 1920.

Dearest li'l' Alling,

. . . I have enjoyed the Victrola [music player] so much! I can whistle almost the whole of the Fifth Symphony, all four movements, and with it I have solaced many a whining hour to sleep. It answers all my questions, the noble, mighty thing, it is 'green pastures and still waters' to my soul. Indeed, without music I should wish to die. Even poetry, Sweet Patron Muse forgive me the words, is not what music is. I find that lately more and more my fingers itch for a piano, and I shall not spend another winter without one. Last night I played for about two hours, the first time in a year, I think, and though most everything is gone enough remains to make me realize I could get it back if I had the guts. People are so dam [sic] lazy, aren't they? Ten years I have been forgetting all I learned so lovingly about music, and just because I am a boob. All that remains is Bach, I find that I never lose Bach. I don't know why I have always loved him so. Except that he is so pure, so relentless and incorruptible, like a principal [sic] of geometry. Did you know I had written a sonnet to Euclid? Does it strike you as funny? It isn't funny, really. Unless, perhaps, I am funny, – which is just possible…

Well, li'l' Agint [sic], this is a long letter when one considers that it is single-spaced.

. . .

I bet you know some new songs, the wedding ceremonial chants of the Igaroots [sic], or some such darned thing, ol' dear.

Lots of love, li'l Alling, till I see you again, which will be soon now.

Edna.

. . .

'YOU MUST BE AWARE OF THE GRAVE CONCERN WITH WHICH ALL SECTIONS OF THE COUNTRY, SOUTH, EAST, WEST AND NORTH HAVE VIEWED YOUR ACTION'

MARIAN ANDERSON'S SUPPORTERS FIGHT FOR HER RIGHT TO SING

Marian Anderson began her career singing in church halls and function rooms in Philadelphia, but ended it performing on the world's most prestigious stages. The path to global success was far from straightforward, however, and Anderson (1897–1993) faced considerable prejudice on account of her race.

In 1925 Anderson got her first 'big break', when she won a prestigious singing competition for which the grand prize was the opportunity to perform in concert with the New York Philharmonic orchestra. Having impressed the audience and critics with her rich contralto voice, she was then invited to perform in small city concert halls, but struggled to gain momentum due to the rampant racial prejudice in America. Her fortunes changed in 1929 when she was awarded a scholarship by the Rosenwald Fund to study in Berlin under the opera singers Sara Charles-Cahier and Geni Sadero; her training prepared the way for a successful singing tour of many of the capitals of Europe, and when Anderson eventually returned to the United States she was famed as a seasoned performer with many a prestigious concert hall tucked under her belt.

As Anderson's popularity grew, so too did the size of the venues she played, but her soaring fame could not protect her from the Jim Crow laws and attitudes of the 1930s, and on her grand tour she was often discriminated against, being refused service in restaurants and hotels. While on tour in 1939, Anderson was earmarked to perform at Constitution Hall in Washington DC, a prestigious venue that could seat up to 4,000. Constitution Hall was owned by the Daughters of the American Revolution (DAR), a patriotic organization whose members claimed a lineage to the original patriots of the American Revolution, and adamantly denied Anderson's application to perform on the basis of their white performers-only policy.

The DAR's rejection of one of the biggest names in American music caused a public outcry, and calls for the DAR to overturn their decision came from all over the country, including from within the White House, where First Lady Eleanor Roosevelt was so outraged by the decision that she resigned her membership from DAR and publicly came to Anderson's support. Eventually it was decided that if the DAR could not be persuaded to reverse their decision, Anderson's supporters would just have to organize their own event. Thus, with the consent of the President and his First Lady, a performance was arranged to be held on the steps of the Lincoln Memorial for Easter Sunday on 9 April 1939. The event, which drew an audience of over 75,000 people and was broadcast to millions, was a resounding success, and now stands as one of the landmark moments in American social history.

Following this historic event, Marion Anderson Citizens Committee (MACC) wrote to the DAR to take them to task for their racism. The group, formed following the DAR's controversial decision, was headed by Charles Hamilton Houston, the law professor integral in undoing the racist 'separate, but equal' policies that allowed state-sponsored segregation. Though Anderson had won her right to sing, it remained the case that the DAR had not overturned its decision. The fight, therefore, was not over, and with this letter the MACC sought to apply continued pressure on the DAR to reconsider its actions.

MARIAN ANDERSON ON STAGE, C. 1950S

From Charles Houston and John Lovell on behalf of The Marian Anderson Citizens Committee to Mrs Roberts and the Daughters of the Revolution, 1939

Mrs. Henry M. Roberts, Jr.,
President-General,
Daughters of the American Revolution,

. . .

13 April 1939

Dear Mrs. Roberts:

Last January, an application was made to the management of Constitution Hall for the use of that auditorium for the presentation for Miss Marian Anderson, world famous contralto, in concert. That request was denied solely on account of the fact that the artist is a Negro.

Your great auditorium with its magnificent representation of the various states, its murals and paintings, is indeed a show-place of the Nation's capital and a real contribution in affording to the citizens of the District a fitting place in which they may enjoy the finest contributors to our American culture.

Without question, Miss Anderson is one of the greatest singers of this generation. America is proud to claim her. The greatest critics have claimed her superb voice and artistry. Millions in America and Europe have thrilled to her songs. Your attitude in this matter well-nigh prevented the citizens of Washington from hearing this marvelous voice.

You must be aware of the grave concern with which all sections of the country, South, East, West and North have viewed your action. It has been branded as a violation of fundamental democratic tenets, and as an expression of bigotry and intolerance, shameful in any group, but hardly conceivable in an organization of descendants of those who fought and died for liberty 165 years ago.

The 75,000 persons who braved chilly spring weather to hear Miss Anderson at Lincoln Memorial on Easter Sunday demonstrated Washington's desire to share in her cultural achievements. The open-air concert, however, did not solve the fundamental issue of the ban on Negro artists in Constitution Hall. The Marian Anderson Citizens Committee and the citizens of Washington wish Miss Anderson to return to Washington in 1940, and want her to sing in the only suitable auditorium.

We, therefore, respectfully request of you:

1. That Constitution Hall be opened to Marian Anderson and other Negro artists.
2. That no reputable and responsible organization be barred from sponsoring a concert in Constitution Hall on account of race.
3. That management of Constitution Hall be instructed to advise the Marian Anderson Citizens Committee as to dates available for concerts by Marian Anderson and other Negro artists in the Concert Season of 1939–1940.

Yours very truly,

CHARLES H. HOUSTON, Chairman
JOHN LOVELL, JR., Secretary

13 April 1939

Mrs. Henry M. Robert, Jr.,
President-General
Daughters of the American Revolution
Continental Hall
17th & D Streets, Northwest
Washington, D.C.

Dear Mrs. Robert:

Last January, an application was made to the management of Constitution Hall for the use of that auditorium for the presentation of Miss Marian Anderson, world famous contralto, in concert. That request was denied solely on account of the fact that the artist is a Negro.

Your great auditorium with its magnificent representation of the various states, its murals and paintings, is indeed a show-place of the Nation's capital and a real contribution in affording to the citizens of the District a fitting place in which they may enjoy the finest contributors to our American culture.

Without question, Miss Anderson is one of the greatest singers of this generation. America is proud to claim her. The greatest critics have acclaimed her superb voice and artistry. Millions in America and Europe have thrilled to her songs. Your attitude in this matter well-nigh prevented the citizens of Washington from hearing this marvelous voice.

You must be aware of the grave concern with which all sections of the country, South, East, West and North have viewed your action. It has been branded as a violation of fundamental democratic tenets, and as an expression of bigotry and intolerance, shameful in any group, but hardly conceivable in an organization of descendants of those who fought and died for liberty 165 years ago.

The 75,000 persons who braved chilly spring weather to hear Miss Anderson at Lincoln Memorial on Easter Sunday demonstrated Washington's desire to share in her cultural achievements. The open air concert, however, did not solve the fundamental issue of the ban on Negro artists in Constitution Hall. The Marian Anderson Citizens Committee and the citizens of Washington wish Miss Anderson to return to Washington in 1940, and want her to sing in the only suitable auditorium.

We, therefore, respectfully request of you:

1. That Constitution Hall be opened to Marian Anderson and other Negro artists.
2. That no reputable and responsible organization be barred from sponsoring a concert in Constitution Hall on account of race.
3. That the management of Constitution Hall be instructed to advise the Marian Anderson Citizens Committee as to dates available for concerts by Marian Anderson and other Negro artists in the Concert Season of 1939-1940.

Yours very truly,

CHARLES H. HOUSTON, Chairman

JOHN LOVELL, JR., Secretary

THE MARIAN ANDERSON PAPERS (UNIVERSITY OF
PENNSYLVANIA), SUPPORTERS [ARRANGED ALPHABETICALLY]
M-W: MARIAN ANDERSON CITIZENS COMMITTEE], MS. COLL
200 BOX 412 ITEM 2C

'COMPOSERS MUST STOP FOLLOWING TRENDS LIKE A GROUP OF POLITICAL OPPORTUNISTS. THEY MUST LEAD PEOPLE TO FAITH IN MANKIND AND IN A GOOD FUTURE'

JOHN DONALD ROBB'S VISION FOR THE SOUND OF POST-WAR MUSIC

As the Allied forces edged ever closer to overcoming the Axis powers of Germany and Japan, the thoughts of many began to drift towards the world they would like to see arise out of the death and destruction that had gripped the world for the past four years. Beyond political and economic aspirations, matters of culture formed an important facet, and particularly what role music had to play in this new dawn. Seeking answers to such a question, a man by the name of Frank Colapinto decided to write a letter to the American composer and musicologist John Donald Robb (1892–1989), to get his opinion.

In his reply, Robb's thoughts were immediately drawn to the last time the world had been in just such a situation, following the conclusion of the First World War. With hindsight, Robb lamented the urgency there had been to leave the old world behind and embrace something new – a desire embodied by the rise of the modernist movement. While an understandable mindset, Robb believed it had proved detrimental to the status of 'serious', or art, music, by making it insular and introspective. Now, with the hope of peace finally on the horizon, it was time for art music to step down from its lofty pedestal and restore its position as the voice of society.

Such a democratic vision for the future of music was indicative of Robb's work as a musicologist. Over the course of the 1940s and 1950s Robb spent much of his time roaming the countryside of New Mexico recording and transcribing the folk tunes of the indigenous population, amassing over 3,000 recordings. It was in this music that Robb felt the heart of the local people resided, and he drew great inspiration from the sounds he heard.

Tradition was not Robb's sole interest, however, and he embraced the new with the same fervour as the old. In 1965, for instance, at the age of 73, he became one of the first composers to embrace the Moog Synthesiser, and he would compose over 60 pieces using the new gadget.

A letter such as this neatly reflects the blueprint that would guide Robb in his career as a musician. By his mantra, the success of music lay in a balance which embraced both tradition and innovation in equal measure.

From John Donald Robb to Frank Colapinto, 1944

New York City, January 27, 1944

Dear Mr. Colapinto:

I am happy to send you my thoughts on the two questions which you have submitted to me as follows:

1. What should post-war music be like?
In answering this question let me state my feeling that the music which followed the last war *followed* the spirit of the times. It was full of harshness, bitterness, novelty. The world was seeking salvation in something new. 'Try anything!' was the watchword and we saw a generation of disillusioned experimenters frantically seeking happiness in developing new material things, in new social experiments. Music followed the trend. It did *not* lead. Hence we had an almost psychopathic emphasis on novelty (which was unfortunately confused with originality) and the slightest similarity between a new work and the work of any previous composer or even the use of any traditional approach was condemned by all those whose voices reached farthest. The result – composers have been composing for composers, critics and conductors and the public has reacted by demanding less of this 'modern' music in our concert halls or by turning to popular music – a field in which oddly enough conservatism has prevailed. I do not speak here of orchestration – a field in which the jazz boys have experimented more boldly than the composers of serious music.

In considering what music should be like after this war I want to say that disillusionment was natural. What was not natural was the result. A serious approach to the problem would have studied that past, holding fast to those things which are good in our tradition and seeking merely to supplant what was bad with something new and better. Instead the prevailing sentiment was revolutionary, 'Let us destroy all loyalty to tradition and start with totally new "inventions" like the twelve-tone technique' said the spokesmen. Well, it didn't work. The public would not come along. A revolution had failed. The mind could not create great music without the heart.

Now – after this war composers must stop *following* trends like a group of political opportunists. They must lead people to faith in mankind and in a good future. They must first of all reaffirm their faith in the great traditions of the past thus again reaching a common meeting place with the public. Let the originality of the composer assert itself in a language which can reach out to all men here and now – and not merely to a hypothetical generation yet to be born. Frankly, I think I see that the tide has already set that way. – Just as our cynical college men of five years ago have found a new loyalty to their country which swept away their corroding sophistries, so our composers are beginning to have the courage again to write in a manner that sounds like music even to the uninitiate.

2 . Who among the living lead to light and in what works?
Stravinsky – *Fire Bird* –. Even this great genius has apparently become ashamed of the traditional elements upon which he built such great works as this.

Hindemith – *Mathis der Maler, Kleine Kammermusik, Viola Sonata, Acht Stücke* for Strings.

Prokofieff [*sic*] – Classical Symphony. In a sense he has been truer to himself than any other great composer.

Shostakovich – First Symphony. Here is a man of very uneven performance. Of late he betrays great faults – even so a great figure.

Now for the Americans –

Deems Taylor – He has created some fine music like the music for the play *Casanova* – and his *Looking-Glass Suite*.

Aaron Copland – One of the obscuranti [*sic*] he still does produce things like *Billy the Kid* in which he actually lets you recognize American folk tunes.

Douglas Moore – His Village Music is I think a really fine work.

. . .

Sincerely yours,

J. D. Robb

'I WILL BE HERE FOR AS LONG AS IT TAKES TO GET THE CREDENTIALS OF A FEDERAL AGENT'

ELVIS PRESLEY UPHOLDS THE LAW

On the morning of 21 December, 1970, Elvis Presley, the King of rock 'n' roll, arrived unannounced at the gates of the White House with a six-page letter addressed to the President of the United States.

The letter, which Presley (1935–77) had written on the plane journey from Los Angeles to Washington DC, laid out the star's concerns for the future of his beloved country. The United States, in Presley's opinion, was rapidly falling into the grip of 'counterculture' ideologies, groups and activities, and he saw it as his duty to do what he could, in his public position, to defend the values of his homeland.

Having risen to international stardom in 1956 with the release of his number-one hit 'Heartbreak Hotel', Presley had spent many years as the face and voice of youth culture in the US. He was a cultural phenomenon in himself, generating a dedicated following and celebrity image thus far unprecedented; by the end of the 1960s Presley had starred in movies and TV specials, won several Grammys and other prestigious awards, and scored 18 number-one hit singles.

Presley felt he was uniquely placed to tackle the counterculture threats of the 1970s – namely drugs and Communism. His offer was simple: all the President needed to do was bestow upon him the office of Federal Agent, and he would set to work rooting out the anti-American insurgents who threatened to undermine the country.

The letter was received by Richard Nixon's aide, Egil 'Bud' Krogh. Krogh was a huge fan of Elvis and, rather than just pass on the letter to the President, he decided to arrange a meeting between the two of them for the very same day. What followed was one of the most fantastical episodes in the history of music.

The meeting began with Presley presenting the President with a gift in the form of an engraved Colt 45 pistol (a prized piece from Presley's personal collection), after which the two men sat down to discuss the topics raised in his letter. As it turned out, the President and the King had more in common than one might have thought. Nixon was himself a gifted musician: he could play five instruments (piano, saxophone, clarinet, accordion and violin) and in 1962 had even played his own composition on Jack Paar's *Tonight* show. This was the Cold War era, and Nixon shared many of Presley's anxieties. Ever mindful of the Communist threat to America, he also expressed concern at the rise in recreational drug use alongside the hippy movement, a problem he blamed in part on the Beatles.

In exchange for the pistol, the President gifted Elvis an honorary badge from the Bureau of Narcotics and Dangerous Drugs; since the King had been an avid collector of police badges for many years, this would be the crowning jewel of his collection.

PRESIDENT NIXON AND ELVIS PRESLEY POSE FOR A PHOTOGRAPH
IN THE OVAL OFFICE OF THE WHITE HOUSE, 1970

From Elvis Presley to President Richard Nixon, 1970

21 December 1970

Dear Mr President,

First I would like to introduce myself. I am Elvis Presley and admire you and have Great Respect for your office. I talked to Vice-President Agnew in Palm Springs three weeks ago and expressed my concern for our country. The Drug Culture, the Hippie Elements, the SDS, Black Panthers, etc do <u>not</u> consider me as their enemy or as they call it, the Establishment. <u>I call it America and</u> I love it. Sir, I can and will be of any service that I can to help the country out. I have no concerns or motives other than helping the country out. So, I wish not to be given a title or an appointed position. I can and will do more good if I were made a federal agent at large and I will help out by doing it my way through communications with people of all ages. First and foremost, I am an entertainer, but all I need is the federal credentials. I am on the plane with Sen. George Murphy and we have been discussing the problems that our Country is faced with. Sir, I am staying at the Washington hotel, Room 505-506-507. I have 2 men who work with me by the name of Jerry Schilling and Sonny West. I am registered under the name of Jon Burrows. I will be here for as long as it takes to get the credentials of a federal agent. I have done an in-depth study of drug abuse and Communist Brainwashing Techniques and I am right in the middle of the whole thing, where I can and will do the most good. I am glad to help just so long as it is kept very Private. You can have your staff or whomever call me anytime today, tonight or tomorrow. I was nominated this coming year one of America's Ten most outstanding young men. That will be in January 18 in my home town of Memphis, Tenn.

I am sending you a short autobiography about myself so you can better understand this approach. I would love to meet you just to say hello if you're not to [*sic*] busy.

Respectfully,

Elvis Presley

PS I believe that you, Sir, were one of the Top Ten Outstanding Men of America also.

I have a personal gift for you also which I would like to present to you and you can accept it or I will keep it for you until you can take it.

ELVIS PRESLEY'S LETTER TO PRESIDENT RICHARD NIXON, WHITE HOUSE CENTRAL FILES: SUBJECT FILES: EX HE 5-1; NIXON PRESIDENTIAL MATERIALS STAFF; NATIONAL ARCHIVES AND RECORDS ADMINISTRATION

'IT IS SURELY NO FUNCTION OF THE BBC TO TRANSMIT LANGUAGE WHICH, AS SHOWN IN A RECENT COURT CASE, IS STILL CLASSED AS OBSCENE'

MARY WHITEHOUSE'S MORAL CRUSADE AGAINST FOUL-MOUTHED POP STARS

Moral panic has been tied up with pop music ever since the blues was labelled 'the devil's music' in the 1920s. As a beacon of youth culture it has made many fear that a sound which glorifies rebellion, excess and hedonism might morally corrupt its listeners, and so undermine the fabric of 'decent' society.

In 1960s Britain, one woman rose to become the leading voice against this perceived depravity afflicting contemporary pop music. Her name was Mary Whitehouse (1910–2001), and she would wage a lifelong campaign against what she described as the 'moral collapse' of the country. Whitehouse would be loved by some, loathed by others, and prove a persistent thorn in the side of the entertainment industry.

Her story began with her launching of the Clean Up TV Campaign in 1964, an initiative targeted at the BBC to protest against permissive programming. She then founded the National Viewers' and Listeners' Association a year later to continue the work of the campaign, and for the next three decades would lead the organization in its effort to defend traditional Christian values.

Lewd music was, in Whitehouse's mind, just one symptom of society's moral decline, and it was imperative that the media be kept in check to make sure the airwaves were kept clean of filth. Of the major broadcasters, Whitehouse deemed the BBC to be one of the worst culprits for broadcasting such material, and over the years she sent it a torrent of correspondence taking it to task whenever she thought it was neglecting its responsibilities to the younger generations.

In June 1972, one such piece of correspondence landed on the desk of Lord Charles Hill of Luton (signed here as Ally Luton), Chairman of the BBC. It was not the first time something like this had dropped into the BBC's post box, and it must have been the cause of some apprehension – or eye rolling – when Luton saw the postmark read the name 'Whitehouse'.

The letter reports Whitehouse's shock at hearing that the Rolling Stones' new album *Exile on Main St.* was being played on the BBC. Though not mentioned directly, the track in question appears to be the opening track, 'Rocks Off', and the four-letter word referred to is likely to be one which starts with F. The court case Whitehouse refers to may be the 1971's *Cohen v. California*, in which a man was found guilty of breaking the peace for wearing an item with the F-word written on it in a courtroom. It is worth noting that the verdict was overturned on appeal, with the judge ruling, rather poetically, that 'one man's vulgarity is another's lyric.'

It is clear from Luton's facetious response that he did not see eye to eye with Whitehouse, though a look at the song's lyrics suggests she had some grounds for concern. The irony is that if Whitehouse had known of the debauchery that pervaded the recording of the album, the four-letter word would have been the least of her concerns.

MARY WHITEHOUSE OUTSIDE THE HOUSE OF COMMONS CARRYING A BUNDLE OF SIGNATURES SUPPORTING HER PETITION, 1965

From Mary Whitehouse to Lord Hill of Luton, 1972

16 June, 1972

Dear Lord Hill,

I understand that the new Rolling Stone's [*sic*] record, 'Exile on Main Street', is being played on Radio 1.

This record uses four-letter words. Although they are somewhat blurred, there is no question about what they are meant to be.

I feel sure you will understand the concern felt about this matter, for it is surely no function of the BBC to transmit language which, as shown in a recent court case, is still classed as obscene. The very fact that this programme is transmitted primarily for young people would, one would have thought, have demanded more, not less, care about what is transmitted.

We would be grateful if you would look into this matter.

Yours sincerely,

(Mrs) Mary Whitehouse

From Lord Hill of Luton to Mary Whitehouse

20th June, 1972

Dear Mrs. Whitehouse,

Thank you for your letter of June 16th in which you state that the tracks from the Rolling Stones record 'Exiles on Main Street' [*sic*], played on Radio I used four-letter words.

I have this morning listened with great care to the tracks we have played on Radio I. I have listened to them at a fast rate, at a medium rate, at a slow rate. Though my hearing is excellent, I did not hear any offending four-letter words whatever.

Could it be that, believing offending words to be there and zealous to discover them, you imagined that you heard what you did not hear?

Yours sincerely

Ally Luton

'THAT'S THE DIFFERENCE BETWEEN YOU AND ME. I DO WHAT I WANT . . . YOU DO WHAT YOU'RE TOLD'

BILLIE JOE ARMSTRONG DEFENDS HIS RIGHT TO MAKE 'BAD' MUSIC

If the blueprint of punk rock were to be summed up in one word, it would be 'unpalatable'. As a counterculture movement, punk is not intended to appeal to the masses. Rather, with its raw and abrasive sound, the genre is meant to disturb, disgust and challenge the popular conventions of society. It is almost ironic, therefore, when one observes the success with which punk music has succeeded in its vulgar mission, as much of so-called 'acceptable' society fails to grasp the concept of unpalatable pop.

A humorous example of such a paradox occurred on 2 December 1996, when one American mother decided to write to the punk band Green Day with some friendly advice on how they might improve the quality of their music, which she felt was entirely unsuitable for her eight-year-old son and his grandad. Perhaps, she dared to suggest, it might be time they tried their hand at making some 'good' music for a change.

By the late 1990s Green Day had risen to become one of the emblematic bands of American punk rock, if not the standard bearers. Though they had formed in 1987, it was not until the release of their third studio album *Dookie* in 1994 that the band achieved their unprecedented commercial success. The album sold over 20 million copies worldwide, and took the band from being an underground novelty to an international sensation. In this instance, however, the concerned listener wrote in response to the tracks on their fourth album *Insomniac*, released in 1995, an album which pioneered a heavier, angrier sound than before. It is unclear which tracks the mother found particular issue with, but one might hazard a guess that the expletive-riddled songs 'Brain Stew' and 'Stuck with Me' might have been at the root of her concern.

Unsurprisingly, the letter failed to have the desired effect. Instead, it prompted a bullish response from Billie Joe Armstrong, the band's chief songwriter and frontman, in which he made clear his motivations for writing the music he and the band produce.

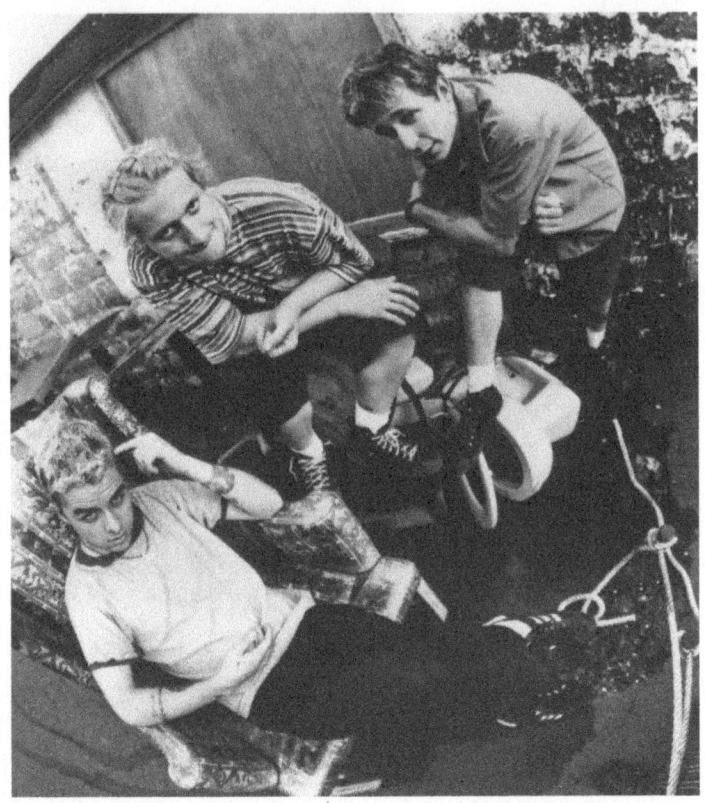

PROMOTIONAL PHOTOGRAPH OF GREEN DAY. FROM LEFT: BILLIE JOE ARMSTRONG, TRÉ COOL AND MIKE DIRNT, 1990S

From Concerned Parent to 'Green Day', 1996

December 2, 1996

To whom it may concern:

I am a parent, and I am very disturbed by the cassette tape my 8 year old son was listening to. His 60 year old grandmother bought it for him as a birthday present and was totally unaware of its explicit content. The store in which she bought it did not have any ticket or color on it to warn parents of the content within. An issue I plan to pursue with the right people.

Isn't it possible to make music anymore? That tape is not something any singer/songwriter should take any pride in at all. It is horrifying and has got to be one of the worst interpretations of an 'artform' that I have ever had the misfortune to hear. I know it is possible for the group to make 'good music' because I have heard them sing before. For example, the song entitled 'When I Come Around' is one of my son's favorites. It's a song that he and his Dad sang together whenever it was on MTV or they were driving in the car together.

Unfortunately, one doesn't have to sing trash to have a following. And if that creates such a following one would do well to wonder exactly what type of people he wants following him! This may do nothing to change the type of music performed or change your views on the art of making music but it helps me to know that there is one less family who will be buying such rubbish and I have a big mouth so I'll make everyone I know aware. That tape is trash, as you can plainly see, and you'll find it enclosed.

Why don't you do something positive and clean up your act!!! Isn't there enough garbage in the world? All the thoughts you are helping to put in the minds of our youths is scary. You have so much influence why not use it for something GOOD?

From Billie Joe Armstrong to 'concerned parent'

. . .

I just received your letter and this is my response.

I don't write music for parents, grandparents, or eight year olds. I write for myself and I'll say anything I damn well please. That's the difference between you and me. I do what I want . . . You do what you're told.

Obviously, we're not on the same planet, let alone the same ball park. I find people like you offensive and it 'helps me' to know no [redacted] you won't be buying any more of our records. Next time, I suggest you do a little research before you purchase such 'rubbish' for your little boy. It might save you a few extra bucks.

Billie Joe and the rest of Green Day

PS
You're right about one thing . . . You do have a big mouth.

'IN TIME, A WILD, DANGEROUS AND RADICAL FORM OF MUSIC CAN TEAR ITS WAY THROUGH THE ICE, TEETH BARED, AND ROCK 'N' ROLL CAN GET BACK TO THE BUSINESS OF TRANSGRESSION'

NICK CAVE ON THE EVOLUTION OF MODERN ROCK
If asked to define rock music, a fan of the genre might give a whole array of answers. Some might reference the psychedelic rock of the 1960s, made famous by bands such as Pink Floyd and the Grateful Dead. Others might describe the dark and grungy era of the 1990s, as popularized by Nirvana and Pearl Jam, or the heavier sounds of bands like Led Zeppelin, AC/DC and Black Sabbath that crept up from basement bars to dominate world stages in the 1970s. Then there are those who would cast their eye further back to the lighter rock 'n' roll sounds of the 1950s that birthed the genre as a whole, referencing icons like Elvis Presley.

Evidently, rock is a genre of music that has been in constant evolution ever since its conception. It ebbs and flows, finding new avenues of sound and purpose as time progresses, adapting to fit – or stand out from – the overarching feel of each passing era. Today, however, some music journalists make the heretical claim that rock is dead. Gone, they argue, are the glory days of heavy instrumentals and searing beats that cut right to the heart. Gone too are the rock stars who made headlines again and again for defying every musical expectation and, occasionally, for their equally expectation-defying bad behaviour.

There is some truth to such claims: the traditional rock star figure has now largely been replaced in youth consciousness by the archetype of the modern pop star – figureheads with ginormous followings of a cult-like nature such as Taylor Swift, Billie Eilish, Justin Bieber and Beyoncé. The way we listen to music has also changed, as streaming platforms have made music more accessible than ever, and unknown artists can go viral overnight with just one hit, as opposed to the graft of starting out on the pubs-and-clubs circuit that was often required to make it big before the advent of social media.

If you ask an icon of the rock scene for their opinion on the state of modern rock, however, you might receive a more nuanced answer. This is exactly what happened when two fans wrote to Nick Cave in 2019 to ask the rock veteran what he really thought of the state of modern rock music. What followed was a considered and pensive response crafted from four decades of experience on the rock 'n' roll scene. While some may be eager to spit on the grave of rock music, Cave sees the genre in evolution: not dead but dormant, and awaiting its next big transformation.

NICK CAVE PERFORMING WITH THE BAD SEEDS AT GLASTONBURY
FESTIVAL, 1998

From Nick Cave to Dylan and Jason, 2019

Dear Dylan and Jason,

Rock music has lurched and shuddered its way through its varied and tumultuous history and somehow managed to survive. It is within the very nature of rock 'n' roll to mutate and to transform — to die so it can live again. This churning is what keeps the whole thing moving forward. As musicians we are always in danger of becoming obsolete and superseded by the next generation's efforts, or by the world itself and its big ideas. Not so long ago the big idea in the world was freedom of expression. It looks like the new big idea is moralism. Will rock music survive this one? We shall see.

My feeling is that modern rock music, as we know it, has anyway been ailing for some time now. It has become afflicted with a kind of tiredness and confusion and faint-heartedness, and no longer has the stamina to fight the great battles that rock music has always fought. It seems to me there is little new or authentic, as it becomes safer, more nostalgic, more cautious and more corporate.

As far as rock music goes, I think that the new moral zealotry that is descending upon our culture could actually be a good thing. Maybe, it is exactly what rock 'n' roll needs at this moment in time. Contemporary rock music no longer seems to have the fortitude to contend with these enemies of the imagination, these enemies of art – and in this present form perhaps rock music isn't worth saving. The permafrost of puritanism could be the antidote for the weariness and nostalgia that grips it. Perhaps a painful reckoning is needed – a great crushing of creativity that descends and lays its self-righteous ice across art – so that in time, a wild, dangerous and radical form of music can tear its way through the ice, teeth bared, and rock 'n' roll can get back to the business of transgression.

Transgression is fundamental to the artistic imagination, because the imagination deals with the forbidden. Go to your record collection and mind-erase those who have led questionable lives and see how much of it remains. It is the artist who steps beyond the accepted social boundaries who will bring back ideas that shed new light on what it means to be alive. This is, in fact, the artist's duty – and sometimes this journey is accompanied by a certain dissolute behaviour, especially in rock 'n' roll. In fact, the nature of rock 'n' roll is dissolute. Sometimes an individual's behaviour is purely malevolent, and this surely needs to be exposed for what it is – and we must make a personal choice as to whether or not we engage with their work.

However, in the world of ideas the sanctimonious have little or no place. Art must be wrestled from the hands of the pious, in whatever form they may come – and they are always coming, knives out, intent on murdering creativity. At this depressing time in rock 'n' roll, though, perhaps they can serve a purpose, perhaps rock music needs to die for a while, so that something powerful and subversive and truly monumental can rise up out of it.

Love, Nick

COPYRIGHT ACKNOWLEDGEMENTS

This book would not have been possible without the generosity of the rights holders who have granted us permission to include the letters in this volume. All relevant rights holders have been credited in the lists below. We have made every possible effort to trace rights holders to obtain their permission to include copyright material. We sincerely apologize for any inadvertent errors or omissions from the following lists, and will endeavour to correct mistakes in subsequent editions.

FACSIMILES

Enrico Caruso to Ada Giachetti, 4 November 1897: from the James Drake collection.

Teresa Carreño to Regina Watson, 5 January 1913: Library of Congress, MacDowell Colony Records (MSS55012).

George Handel to Charles Jennens, 1749: Handel, George Frideric. Letter from George Frideric Handel to Charles Jennens, 30 Sept., 1749. https://www.loc.gov/item/musmolden.2774/.

Ludwig van Beethoven to Carl and Johann Beethoven, 6 October 1802: public domain, sourced from Wikimedia Commons.

Edvard Grieg to a fan, 29 June 1892: Courtesy of Private Collection/Christies Images/Bridgeman Images.

Elvis Presley to Richard Nixon, 21 December 1970: Elvis Presley's Letter to President Richard Nixon, White House Central Files: Subject Files: EX HE 5-1; Nixon Presidential Materials Staff; National Archives and Records Administration.

The Marian Anderson Committee to Mrs. Roberts and the Daughters of the Revolution, 13 April 1939: Sourced from the Marian Anderson Papers (University of Pennsylvania), Supporters [arranged alphabetically] M-W: Marian Anderson Citizens Committee, Ms. Coll 200 box 412 item 2c.

LETTERS

Chapter One

Christoph Willibald Gluck to Jean-François de La Harpe, 1777: sourced
from *The Musician's World: Letters of the Great Composers*, edited by Hans
Gal, translated by Daphne Woodward (Thames & Hudson, 1965).
Translation © the Estate of Daphne Woodward.

Frédéric Chopin to his family, 12 August 1829: translated by Arthur
Hedley. Sourced from *Selected Correspondence of Fryderyk Chopin*,
collected and annotated by Bronislaw Edward Sydow, translated by
Arthur Hedley (Heinemann, 1962).

Pyotr Ilyich Tchaikovsky to Édouard Colonne, 25 December 1876: ©
Brett Langston, www.tchaikovsky-research.net.

Amy Winehouse school report, 1995: copyright © Chas Newkey-
Burden 2011. First published in the UK by John Blake, an imprint of
Bonnier Books UK Ltd.

Chapter Two

Jean-Philippe Rameau to Antoine Houdar de la Motte, 25 October
1727: Translated by Daphne Woodward. Sourced from *The Musician's
World: Letters of the Great Composers*, edited by Hans Gal, translated by
Daphne Woodward (Thames & Hudson, 1965).

Richard Wagner to King Ludwig II of Bavaria, 6 November 1864:
Translation © Stewart Spencer and Barry Millington.

Arthur Honegger to his parents, 28 April 1915: From: *Arthur Honegger*
by Harry Halbreich (Amadeus Press, 1999). Translation © Roger
Nichols, used with permission.

Herbert Howells to Leonard Howells, 19 January 1917: Permission of
the Herbert Howells Trust.

Leoš Janáček to Kamila Stösslová, 1927: Used with permission of
Princeton University Press, from *Intimate Letters: Leoš Janáček to Kamila
Stösslová*, edited by John Tyrrell (2014); permission conveyed through
Copyright Clearance Center, Inc.

Chapter Three

Hildegard of Bingen to Prelates of Mainz, 1178: *Women in Music: An
Anthology of Source Readings from the Middle Ages to the Present*, edited by
Carol Neuls-Bates, pp. 18–19. © 1996 Carol Neuls-Bates. Reprinted
with permission of Johns Hopkins University Press.

Opera in Letters and Documents, collected and translated by Hans Busch (University of Minnesota Press, 1978). Copyright 1978 by the University of Minnesota. Translation © the Estate of Edward Downes.

Enrico Caruso to Ada Giachetti, 4 November 1897: Translated by Valentina Gosetti, by permission of James Drake.

Leonard Bernstein to Aaron Copland, 22 March 1938: Excerpted from *The Leonard Bernstein Letters*, edited by Nigel Simeone © 2013 Nigel Simeone. Letters by Leonard Bernstein © Amberson Holdings LLC. Reproduced with permission of the Licensor through PLSclear.

Arnold Schoenberg to Olin Downes, 21 December 1948: Used with permission of Rowman & Littlefield Publishing Group, Inc., from Arnold Schoenberg Correspondence: A Collection of Translated and Annotated Letters Exchanged with Guido Adler, Pablo Casals, Emanuel Feuermann, and Olin Downes, edited by Egbert M. Ennulat, 1991. permission conveyed through Copyright Clearance Center, Inc.

Chapter Six

Gustav Mahler to Alma Schindler, 19 December 1901: Translated by Antony Beaumont. Reproduced by permission of Faber & Faber Ltd.

Zitkála-Šá to Carlos Montezuma, 23 June 1913: Used with permission of Brill from: *Zitkala-Ša: Letters, Speeches, and Unpublished Writings, 1898–1929*, edited by Tadeusz Lewandowski, (2017) pp. 100–2.; permission conveyed through Copyright Clearance Centre, Inc.

Janis Joplin to Dorothy and Seth Joplin, 6 June 1966: Reproduced from *Love, Janis* by Laura Joplin (Villard Books, 1992) with permission from Fantality Corporation. © the Estate of Janis Joplin.

John Lydon to Martin, 1978: © John Lydon, reproduced with permission.

Elton John to 'cocaine', 10 August 1990: Excerpt from *ME: ELTON JOHN* by Elton John. Copyright © 2019 by HST Global Limited. Reprinted by permission of Henry Holt and Company. All Rights Reserved. Excerpt from *Me: Elton John*, first published in 2019 by Macmillan, an imprint of Pan Macmillan. Reproduced by permission of Macmillan Publishers International Limited Copyright. © HST Global Limited 2019.

IMAGES

Edward Elgar: Pictorial Press/Alamy Stock Photo
Teresa Carreño: Penta Springs Limited/Alamy Stock Photo
Arthur Honegger: Lebrecht Music & Arts/Alamy Stock Photo
Herbert Howells: Lebrecht Music & Arts/Alamy Stock Photo
Leoš Janáček: Heritage Image Partnership Ltd/Alamy Stock Photo

Chapter Three
Magnus Aurelius Senator Cassiodorus: Realy Easy Star/Alamy Stock
    Photo
Hildegard of Bingen: Art Reserve/Alamy Stock Photo
Arnold Schoenberg: Science History Images/Alamy Stock Photo
Michael Tippett: Keystone Press/Alamy Stock Photo
John Coltrane: Album/Alamy Stock Photo

Chapter Four
George Handel: CBW/Alamy Stock Photo
Christoph Willibald Gluck: GL Archive/Alamy Stock Photo
Joseph Haydn: Pictorial Press Ltd/Alamy Stock Photo
Fanny Mendelssohn: IanDagnall Computing/Alamy Stock Photo
Clara Schumann: IanDagnall Computing/Alamy Stock Photo
Edvard Grieg: Lebrecht Music & Arts/Alamy Stock Photo
Sergei Prokofiev: IanDagnall Computing/Alamy Stock Photo
Woody Guthrie: Pictorial Press Ltd/Alamy Stock Photo
Michael Tippett: Lebrecht Music & Arts/Alamy Stock Photo
Syd Barrett: INTERFOTO/Alamy Stock Photo

Chapter Five
Giacomo Puccini: GL Archive/Alamy Stock Photo
Giuseppe Verdi: CBW/Alamy Stock Photo
Enrico Caruso: Allstar Picture Library Limited/Alamy Stock Photo
Ethel Smyth: Pictorial Press Ltd/Alamy Stock Photo
Leonard Bernstein: Keystone Press/Alamy Stock Photo

Chapter Six
Ludwig van Beethoven: Pictorial Press Ltd/Alamy Stock Photo
Robert Schumann: IanDagnall Computing/Alamy Stock Photo
Jenny Lind: Pictorial Press Ltd/Alamy Stock Photo

Gustav Mahler: GRANGER-Historical Picture Archive/Alamy Stock Photo

Zitkála-Šá: IanDagnall Computing/Alamy Stock Photo

Janis Joplin: Keystone Press/Alamy Stock Photo

John Lydon: Associated Press/Alamy Stock Photo

Elton John: David Hickes/Alamy Stock Photo

Chapter Seven

Gustav Holst: GRANGER-Historical Picture Archive/Alamy Stock Photo

Edward Elgar: Science History Images/Alamy Stock Photo

Marian Anderson: Everett Collection Inc/Alamy Stock Photo

Elvis Presley and Richard Nixon: White House Photo/Alamy Stock Photo

Mary Whitehouse: PA Images/Alamy Stock Photo

Green Day: Pictorial Press Ltd/Alamy Stock Photo

Nick Cave: Photo: Edd Westmacott/Alamy Stock Photo

ABOUT THE EDITORS

JAMES DRAKE

© Georgiana Chitea

James Drake is Founder of the Drake Foundation, the Drake Calleja Trust, Future Medicine Limited and Of Lost Time.

Some years ago James acquired the letter archive of the former great tenor Enrico Caruso. His first instinct was to show it to the greatest contemporary lyric tenor, Joseph Calleja; he was inspired by the tenor's deep emotion at seeing the manuscripts. This crystallized James's passion for connecting to the past through the power of personal historical correspondence and led him to establish Of Lost Time Ltd, a name inspired by his experience of handling an original draft for a portion of Proust's great novel, *In Search of Lost Time*.

To learn more, visit his website at www.JamesDrake.com

Of Lost Time Ltd: www.oflosttime.com

EDWARD SMYTH

Edward Smyth is a writer, editor and professional fundraiser. He holds under- and post-graduate degrees in music and an MA in theology from Durham University, and a further master's degree in criminology from Oxford. Edward is the Chair of Sing Inside, a small charity delivering singing workshops in prisons, and is Head of Development at the Prison Reform Trust. This is his second co-edited volume in the Letters for the Ages series, following on from *Behind Bars: Letters from History's Most Famous Prisoners*.

INDEX